Praise for PROFIT Y

Dave Fuller has written a handbook for small business owners. In plain English, this book delivers powerful stories and direct advice that de-mystifies business and will put more money in your pocket. A powerful read, and full of simple action steps.

Robert Sher
author of *Mighty Midsized Companies* & a veteran CEO

Profit Yourself Healthy, by Dave Fuller, is a must-read for anyone who is a small business owner. Dave gives a great overview of business effectiveness fundamentals, along with exercises to make his instruction personal for you. The true stories interwoven make this an interesting and fun read, in addition to being instructive. This is a great book for business people and a great gift for someone you know who wants to do it right!

Jon Denney
President, Professional Business Coaches Alliance – USA
Author of *Unstuck*

Profit Yourself Healthy will help you in every aspect of your business, big or small. Dave has had a long career as a successful businessman and his coaching methods are proven and effective. I know this because Dave has coached me in several key areas of my business and I have seen positive results. If you don't have Dave as a business coach, the next best thing is to get a copy of Profit Yourself Healthy and use it. I know it will help you.

Bruce W. Cole
Publisher, CNHR Magazin

This is my new go-to resource book for my clients. Dave Fuller has managed to clearly and practically capture the major issues that my clients are facing and he offers down to earth, easily accessible advice to help owners turn their situation around. I love the way that Dave takes a whole systems approach - from the health of the owner to the health of the business and even the health of the family. It is so important today, when we are all bombarded with information that can be overwhelming, that we can find practical advice delivered in a manageable, interesting and enticing format. Well done Dave, this is definitely a book for my client Christmas list.

Lisë Stewart
President and Founder
Galliard International and the Galliard Family Business Advisor Institute

PROFIT YOURSELF HEALTHY

DAVE FULLER, MBA, CPBC

Profit Yourself Healthy

Tellwell Talent

www.tellwell.ca

ISBN

978-1-77302-107-2 (Paperback)

978-1-77302-108-9 (eBook)

This book is dedicated to Margaret, Emily, Isabel, Sophia, and Caleb, my joys in life!

For small business owners who are working so hard to make a difference in the world and in the lives of their customers and families.

Table of Contents

Introduction

"Business is about building a sustainable way of making the impact that you care about making" - Danny Iny

If you are the owner of a small- to medium-sized business with between 0-50 employees and are reading this book, chances are that you would like to make more profits. In reality, 60% of businesses only make a small amount of money or are not profitable at all, according to research by the National Federation of Independent Business (NFIB, 2013). 97% of businesses report less than $1 million in sales and owner income of less than $50,000 (Hall, Jumpstart Your Business Brain). As business owners, we constantly ask ourselves, "How can I make my business work? How can I grow my business to a point where I can get my investment out and actually make some real money?" We have all been there. I know what it is like to struggle in business. I have felt the shame and discouragement that comes along with not knowing how to make a business work and losing money. I also know what it is like to make healthy sustained profits and use those profits to make my life easier and enrich the lives of those around me. The millions of dollars in profits that my various business endeavours have generated have not been solely as a result of my own work. If it weren't for the work of my dedicated staff; support and ideas from partners and investors; and the mentors, teachers, coaches, friends, and family I have been blessed with, I would have failed. I have felt the feeling of success and the thrill of having a business run smoothly. I know the effects of business stress on my health and have seen its effects on others. It's for this reason that I wanted to write this book for small business owners. I want to help business owners like you have a clearer picture of what works and how to implement proven strategies into your business so that you can be successful and healthier. If you are ready for your business profits to grow, this book is for you!

What is Profit? Before we get into this book we need to be clear about what we are talking about. Profit is usually defined as the difference between our selling price and our costs. I would define this as gross profit. Profit in terms of small business is defined as what is left over after our expenses are paid. It is money that can be used by the owners to either re-invest in the business or use as they see fit for their personal lives. To be even clearer, profit should not include regular wages and benefits for the owner who is working in the business. Owner wages and benefits need to be separated from profit because that owner would be making a similar amount working in another organization. (This is called an opportunity cost). **Therefore, profit is the amount left over after all the business expenses and the owner's regular management salary have been paid.**

What Would You Do With More Profits? If your business generated more money, what would you do with the profits? Most business owners would love to have more profits; not just for the money, but for what that profit and that money could do for them. Increased profits can buy them time to spend with children and grandchildren, time to relax after years of toiling away at their businesses, time to pursue other interests or dreams. Increased profits can allow them to properly plan for retirement, pay off their mortgage, or save for their children's education. Many business owners I know would love to have more time and money to give to charity and the community. The truth is that being in business is often so stressful that it breaks up families and causes health concerns. Lack of profits is often the largest contributing factor to that stress.

Why I Wrote This Book: After 27 years of owning and running my own businesses and enjoying the profits that those businesses had generated, I decided that I wanted more. **I wanted to help others be successful so they could reap the benefits of being a business owner. I wanted them to enjoy a lifestyle which includes healthy profitability and happiness.** For my new mission to be successful, I knew that I needed more information, more knowledge, and a better base to add credibility. I enrolled in the Master of Business Administration program at the University of Northern British Columbia, and for the next two years I was taught by great instructors from around the globe. Upon completion of the program (in fact the day after graduation), I flew to Syracuse, New York for an intensive training program to become a professional business coach. I studied with Jon Denny and the Professional Business Coach Alliance (PBCA) and learned more about how I could help business owners achieve success and profitability.

As a result of my education, years of practical knowledge from both successful and not-so-successful business ventures, and from coaching North American and European clients, I have come to understand that the chances of profitability can be greatly increased with some simple concepts which are outlined in this book. This book will show you *how business profits can be good for your body, mind & soul as well as your pocketbook!* **After reading this book you will have a roadmap to make your business profitable. We will explore why many businesses are not profitable and show you how you can turn your business into a cash-generating machine.** Not only that, this book will help you enjoy the fruits of your years of labour.

It will teach you how to increase the value of your business so when you want to sell it, someone will gladly buy! Finally, my hope is that by following this roadmap you will find the excitement to work on your business again and, as a result, have a more fulfilling life with less stress and more enjoyment.

How to Read This Book: You can read this book a number of ways. I suggest that you start at the beginning and read forward; however, you may wish to concentrate on a certain area of your business and just read that chapter. Throughout each chapter there are "**Do It Now!**" sections. This will give you some concrete steps that you can take to move your business forward and make it profitable. If you follow the steps in any of the book chapters, I guarantee that you will make your business more successful and profitable. If not, send me the book back and I will gladly refund your money. I really want you to be successful. By reading this book you will be further on the path to increased profitability, which will lead to your greater happiness.

Health Tips For Business Owners: In addition to more profit, I also want you to be healthy. After working almost 30 years in the health industry, I have come to realize that stress is the underlying cause of 90% of diseases. As business owners we are subjected at times to incredible stress and mental torment. If you are suffering as a result of this, I hope you will find relief in some of the health solutions presented throughout the book.

The Stories: The stories in this book are based on real events and businesses and are used to give examples of what happens in business and to business owners. In many instances, the names and details have been slightly altered to protect the identity and privacy of the business owners involved. The stories of events in my businesses and life are true as I remember them.

To download your *Profit Yourself Healthy* Worksheets go to: www.profityourselfhealthy.com/bookdownloads/

Chapter 1: Why We Need Profits!

"Profit is a financial benefit that is realized when the amount of revenue gained from a business activity exceeds the expenses, costs and taxes needed to sustain the activity. Any profit that is gained goes to the business's owners, who may or may not decide to spend it on the business" - Investopedia

It was approaching midnight when my flight from New York landed. As I waited for my bags after a long week away from home, I noticed an acquaintance:

"Hey Vince, where were you?"

"In Vancouver taking some technical courses. You, Dave?"

"I was in New York taking some coaching courses. I like to say I am semi-retired from the stores now and am coaching successful business owners who are stuck in some aspect of their business. It might be that they are having cash flow

problems, people problems, lack of profitability, or worrying about competition or thinking about exit strategies."

When I mentioned competition and helping successful business owners, Vince's eyes lit up. "I think we should talk," he said. "I am an expert in my field but another company has just turned up in town and I feel threatened. I have never been taught business and I need help."

It turns out that Vince's new competition had scooped one of his key staff members and he was worried that his business might not be sustainable in the long run. The toll of this stress was weighing heavy on him and he dreaded ever having started his business.

A few weeks later we set to work, delving into his business and setting weekly goals to move the business forward. His personal goal was to build a business that was immune to this competition and that could run one day without him being in the building every day. After asking Vince what he would do when he achieved his goals, he responded with three things:

1.   More time for himself,

2.   More money to spend on his family, and

3.   Better relationships as a result of less stress.

After analyzing Vince's business financials, it was apparent that while he had a successful business, there were issues with profitability. After looking at the sales for each month I noticed some month's sales were 30% higher than the others. Vince already knew why. When his staff was following the sales system properly, his business ran at nearly full capacity. However, his new sales person apparently wasn't following the system. Once Vince corrected the problem, sales and profits started to flow. In the second quarter we worked together there was a $36,000 increase in profits; the third quarter was even more. For many small businesses such an increase is significant. Vince met his goals and is now able to take more time off, and boasts to me that he is less stressed. Vince's wife confided in me that the reduction in stress means that he has been much happier at home with the family.

This is a typical example of how increased profits from a small business can change how people feel and how they relate to others. The stress levels that business owners feel when their business is just marginal or losing money can play a significant role in family life and in the health of business owners.

Some say that profits are the only reason that people are in business, but I would disagree. I don't know about you, but I got into business because I had an opportunity for something challenging. There was the thrill of business and the game but also I wanted to make a difference in the lives of others, and to be the one who determined my destiny. Some of my clients are in business because of the reasons below:

- Necessity: They had to because they were a single mother or father needing to provide for their children while working around their kid's schedule.

- Training: Tradespeople or professionals are often in business because that is what is expected in the trade, there are not many options.

- An Idea for a better product or service: Some entrepreneurs developed a product and built a business around the demand for that product.

- Family Business: Some business owners have inherited or taken over the family business

- Unmet Opportunity: Some entrepreneurs like you are opportunity seekers and when they see an unmet opportunity decide to capitalize on it.

While the reasons for getting into business are varied, all business owners hope to have financial security. When things go right, business owners like you and I can make a great income and have the freedom to do what we love both inside and outside our businesses.

While I got into business for the thrill and to make a difference, it took me a while to figure out that I was in business to make profits. My partner Louis, who financed our businesses but was busy making money in land development, would tell me once or twice a year, **"Dave, we are in business to make money!"** For me at that time, like many business owners, **being in business was about the lifestyle, about building something, and about serving my customers.** After building the business for several years (at the age of 29), it was profitable but only marginally. The fact was that I was making more money renovating and flipping houses in the evenings and weekends than I was from the business. To clear my head, I decided to take six months off and travel. I systemized the business so that I had department managers who were responsible for ordering products and the overall success of the company, and I had a great bookkeeper, Rachael. Upon returning from my trip, I decided that if I was going to stay in this business I was going to take it seriously. It's at that point that I began to realize that we needed to make healthy profits to grow the business and to reap the rewards of that work.

A second shift in my relationship with profits took place after we hired a business analyst in the early 1990s from George S. May International to evaluate our store. The contract stated that for $500, the analyst would evaluate the store and make recommendations for improvements, and I would have to be available for a 1-hour period once the report was ready. The analyst investigated our operations, interviewed my staff, and reviewed the financials. His report was critical of almost every aspect of the business, including profit margins. While we were making money, our profit percentage was about ½ of what it should be for similar types of operations. He made it sound like my staff hated me and that if I didn't subscribe to his proposal for $70,000 worth of consulting to fix the problems, I would be in dire straits. Needless to say, after exactly 60 minutes of high-pressure sales tactics, I bid farewell. While I didn't buy into any consulting, I took the recommendations seriously and made the changes suggested. The results took time, but the regularly scheduled staff reviews, changes in margin, and increases in systemization reaped its rewards. Within a year, profits were up and my partners were even happier than ever. The change in my mindset was paramount in the success of the business. The commitment to having a streamlined and profitable business drove the operation to new levels. I believe that there are many business owners out there who are in the same boat. They haven't made the commitment yet to making their business profitable. If this is you, **there is a mental shift that needs to happen for you to understand clearly that you need to make money in your business day in and day out, month over month and year over year!** This book will help you do that.

Today my relationship with profits has changed again.

As I get older, and continue to see healthy profits in my businesses, I see more of the need for business owners to put money away for the future. You need to invest in opportunities that are going to provide you with cash for your future. No one else is going to do that for you. I look at profits as not only a scorecard in the fun game of business but also as something to be shared, shared with those who have helped me earn them as well as those that cannot earn them. What you do with your profits is your own choice, but the evidence is clear: if you do not make money in your business you are not going to have that business for long. Without profits, you are not going to be able to support your staff or your own family. There is a process to achieving profits that can support you in your retirement. The process starts with a clear vision of what you want for your life and your business and ends with your retirement and enjoyment of the fruits of your hard work. That is one of the most compelling reasons for making your business profitable and keeping it profitable.

Profit Yourself Healthy Pyramid

Sit back and relax and share your profits – You have arrived

Have a retirement plan & build investments

Develop a marketing plan

Develop a sales plan

Develop a people plan

Develop a systems plan

Stop the bleeding now

Your strategy to get there

Know what you want and where you want to be

Let's look at some of the other reasons why we need profits.

More Profit = Owners like you can work less: Profits can allow you, the business owner, to cut down on the number of hours you are spending at work and take more time for your family and friends. This doesn't mean going home and talking about business. If your business is running well, leave your business at work. If you haven't noticed, your family and friends do not want to always hear about your problems at your business. They have their own problems and want to talk about themselves or things you have in common. Your business makes profits to provide you with a balanced life. Who wants to be remembered as the guy that worked all the time when you are dead? Use your profits to create balance and spend more time appreciating your family and friends. Yes, there are times when entrepreneurs need to work hard and work long hours. Once you are through this stage of your business, make sure you put the systems that allow you to enjoy the fruits of all that labour into place. If the reason you started a business in the first place was to have a better life for yourself and your family, start enjoying it now. Life is short!

More Profits = Owners like you have less stress: We all have stress in our lives and we all handle it differently. What is stressful for me might not be stressful at all for you and vice versa. When my businesses were in trouble and the bank managers and my partner were calling me on a daily or weekly basis to ask about my cash flow, my stress levels were high. I stopped eating, stopped exercising, was constantly thinking about work, was short with my family and friends, and spent too many hours trying to solve my company's problems. This resulted in people not wanting to be around me because I was engrossed in my difficulties. After long months of hard work and a rollercoaster of trials and errors, setbacks, and small successes, we were able to return to profitability. Once I could see the light at the end of the tunnel and had a couple months of profitability back under my belt, my stress levels dropped. I was able to return to my "normal" self and enjoy again those things I had taken for granted that were happening around me on a daily basis. This book is written so that you can reduce your stress by avoiding similar situations. More profits can greatly reduce the stress related to a struggling business. By keeping your bottom line healthy, you can be healthy too!

More Profits = Owners like you have better health: According to a 2014 study by the American Psychological Association that reviewed stress levels of Americans, 72% of respondents were stressed about money sometime in the last month (American Psychological Association, 2015)! Dr. Gabor Maté, in his bestselling book "*When the Body Says No: The Cost of Hidden Stress*," talks about the relationship between internal and hidden stress and significant health issues, including cancer (Mate, 2004). Having experienced firsthand the effects of long periods of significant stress, I can honestly tell you that when my businesses are making money and my stress levels are low, I have better health. This relationship between profits and health is often overlooked. Healthy profits allow business owners to afford themselves the time they need to exercise and be proactive in looking after their bodies. They are able to afford medical treatments and take the time to do what they need to do to reduce stress with exercise or leisure.

More Profits = Business owners like you can have better relationships: Many business owners can tell you that when they enjoy profits they enjoy them with their family and friends. These profits allow business owners to take memorable vacations, have a guest house or cabin, or buy or build a home where they can be comfortable and cherish loved ones. The key here is that without the profits, business owners like you and I would be working more and spending less time with our family and friends. In fact, the same American Psychological Association survey mentioned above stated that 31% of adults with partners report that money is a significant source of stress (American Psychological Association, 2015). Without profits derived from their business, entrepreneurs are forced to work long hours in order to avoid hiring staff and paying additional wages, which can put pressure on a marriage or relationship. In a study by Dr. Brian Robinson of the University of Northern Carolina, divorce rates among workaholics were 55% compared to only 16% of marriages where the spouse was not a workaholic (Robinson, 1999). When healthy profits are available, business owners will use these profits to better their life and the lives of those around them, and in doing so take the time to build better relationships.

Besides what profits do for business owners, let's also consider what they do for society as a whole!

Healthy Profits = Healthy society: There has been much written about the evils of profit: how the rich are getting richer and the poor are getting poorer, and how the richest 1% of the population own or control 48% of the world's wealth and spend considerable amounts lobbying governments to protect their rights to hoard more money (Oxfam, 2015). This book is not meant to address these discrepancies but to cast light on the fact that the average business owner reading this book right now is definitely not in that 1% and contributing significantly to the communities they are living in. In

November 2011, Rosabeth Moss Kanter wrote a great article titled "How Great Companies Think Differently" that was published in the Harvard Business Review. In that article, Kanter, who spends her life studying "admired and financially successful companies," describes in detail how and why great companies see the necessity for profits. But these companies balance that profit with the view that businesses are vehicles for accomplishing societal improvement (Kanter, 2011 November). Think about your own community and the business owners who have contributed to improvements from their profits. Where would we be today without those contributions by profitable businesses?

Healthy Profits = More jobs: According to Industry Canada, small business (between 1-99 employees) employed 69.7% of the private labour force in Canada, hiring 7.7 million people and contributing 30% of the Gross Domestic Product (GDP). Small business also represented almost 98% of the total number of businesses in Canada (Canada, 2013). The US numbers are much similar. So what does this mean?

1. Small businesses create more jobs on average than medium or large businesses!

2. If companies are profitable, jobs in small businesses can last for long periods of time and provide stability for families and the community.

3. These jobs from small business are in local communities which are not usually in urban business centers where larger companies tend to operate therefore providing character, culture and economic diversity for smaller communities.

4. The jobs in small profitable companies tend to be more stable in times of economic downturns because the smaller companies can operate on less revenue with lower overhead and often have a greater loyalty to their employees who might be friends and family.

5. Finally, small business is more likely to employ people who would tend to be excluded from higher paying government or large corporation jobs. We are talking not only about seniors, but youth and the marginalized, who may only be able to work for a few hours at a time. Think back to your first job. Chances are that it was working for a small business owner who had a franchise, a gas station, a farm, or a grocery store. Without profitable companies, the whole economy slows down.

Healthy Profits = More taxes: A recent study commissioned by the National Federation of Independent Business showed that small businesses often pay almost twice the tax rate of large corporations (Strategies, 2014). The study draws light on the fact that governments are bending to the pressures of large corporations, yet remain blind to the overall contributions and significant taxes paid by small business. Not only do small businesses contribute more in federal taxes, they also contribute more in municipal taxes that go toward their communities. Without profitable businesses these communities run the risk of losing a significant tax base. Taxes are used to build infrastructure like sewers, water lines, roads, and cities. Taxes used wisely can help our underprivileged and fund our government's attempts to make the world a better and safer place.

Healthy Profits = More charity: Look around at who is sponsoring your child's soccer, hockey, or cheer team. Consider who is donating to the advertising in your seniors' newsletters, sponsoring local plays and arts shows, and investing in your local schools. Without small profitable businesses, the landscape in your local community would be much different. To ensure that we have business owners that can afford to be charitable, we need to ensure that the businesses are profitable first, and that those profits are healthy.

Healthy Profits = More innovation: It is a proven fact that small business drives innovation. Look at Apple, Microsoft, or almost any other large company you see today. Chances are that they were started by a couple of people with an idea that they could do something better than what was in the market already. Many times, the innovation created by small business owners causes shifts in demand for products or services through their creativity and imagination. This innovation is driven by a desire for profits. Often, as companies grow, they lose the need and desire to remain innovative. Sometimes companies are able to create a culture that is conducive to creativity as they grow, but many times the business turns to one of protecting market share rather than creating new markets. Profits from small business owners reinvested in their business or invested in new businesses are often the seeds that enable the economy to grow and flourish.

The fact is, you got into business to make money and have a life. Not making a profit means that you are wasting opportunities to have less stress and make more money working for someone else. You need to commit to making your business profitable by exploring opportunities and working in concrete ways towards ensuring that profit.

Why owners need profits

Less Stress

Less Work

Better health

Better relationships

Your retirement

Take 5 minutes and write down 10 things you could do with more profits from your business. Think about how these things will change your life and the lives of those around you. Consider how your profits could make the world a better place.

1.   6.

2.   7.

3.   8.

4.   9.

5.   10.

Health Tips For Business Owners: Get Your Brain Remembering

Need to remember more about what you are reading? Keep some rosemary handy and sniff it. Research show that this can actually help you remember! A tried-and-true practical method is making notes. Don't be afraid to make your own notes right in the book or underline things that are important to you! Making notes will also reduce your worry about forgetting things. Lists help the brain and are a proven way to effective time management.

Chapter 2: Is Your Business Under Attack? Stop the Bleeding!

Getting control of your business

It was a cold dark night in October 2015, and I was in the bush three hours away from the nearest hospital, as I was to later realize. The black bear was big and predatory, and I was awoken by its movement in our camp that night, knocking over something in the food tent located just a few feet away from my tent. Neil and I, who weren't hunters but were along for the adventure, were in one wall tent (the kind often used in the bush by hunters or tree planters). Paul, his son Jonah, our other friend Dave, and his son Owen slept in the other with the guns.

Paul had also been awoken by the noise and rolled out of his cot by the tent door to grab his flashlight and his rifle. As he turned the light on the bear immediately rushed him. In its ferociousness the bear bit a chunk of flesh the size of your fist out of Paul's lower leg. Kicking and yelling I could hear Paul shout for Dave to shoot the bear. A few seconds later I heard the gunshot, then the yelling: "*You shot my arm, my arm is gone.*"

Jumping to my feet intent to help, I grabbed the flashlight, woke Neil, and opened the tent door. As I shone the light out of the tent towards the other tent, I could see the reflection of the bear's eyes as it lumbered out of the hunter's tent and came directly towards me, brushing my leg as it came into my tent. A few more minutes of intense excitement followed in which the bear emerged out of my tent and took a few wounded steps towards the food tent before turning and plodding back into Paul and Dave's tent where it was finally killed.

Synopsis: There are times in the life of every business operation when the business comes under attack. This is stressful for the owners who might feel like they have been mauled. Often, these attacks happen when we least expect them. This chapter will give you some ideas about what you need to do if your business is under attack, discuss some of the fears that owners have, and clearly show you what needs to happen to stop the bleeding.

Attacks on a Business

Dr. Gordon had been mauled up pretty good by two different attacks on his business, which he hadn't seen coming either. The first wound was when the associate he hired to help in the business, whom he trusted and trained, left with one of his key staff and some customers. If that wasn't enough, the big bite came only a couple of months later when he realized that the theft of a large amount of money by a trusted employee had taken a chunk out of his bank balance and cash flow.

Dr. Gordon was in a state of shock when I came on the scene. He had stopped the financial bleeding himself by firing the employee who had been feasting on his business. Yet he was shaken up. Just like many business owners in similar situations, he was discouraged and unsure of his ability to run his practice like a business. I came on board to help him face the threat of his former associate competing with his practice, and we quickly got down to work. We looked at what was going right in the practice, what his strengths were, what he liked doing, and what was working for him. We analysed his competition and laser focused his business in profitable areas. Fortunately, Dr. Gordon had a wonderful reputation for compassionate care and service, many referrals, and some great systems. Over the next several months, we optimized the business by ensuring that his sales machine was oiled properly and his customer service was polished. He was able to trim some more expenses and add another revenue stream. Today, Dr. Gordon's business is significantly more profitable than it was just a year before. Plus, he has regained his confidence and has a renewed interest in keeping his practice healthy and profitable.

Business Failure - Times when my businesses were bleeding

My very first business venture, besides selling lemonade, was selling worms with my brothers, and it was disastrous. At the age of 13, our family lived on a small acreage outside of the city limits. My brothers, Rob and Paul, were close in age and always looking for new exciting things. This particular summer, we needed money to go to the county fair. It just so happened that we came across an ad in the "Buy and Sell" titled <u>Worms Wanted</u>. The ad read, "We buy worms, $15.00 per thousand." In 1976, $15 was a lot of money! It didn't take us long to respond to the ad. We knew where the worms were, and they were in our yard. In fact, we made the call and went right out to our barnyard and dug up worms. Five thousand worms to be exact. We sweated in the sun and counted every one of those worms dropping them each into a bucket with a lid so they wouldn't escape. Seeing as it was quite hot that day we thought that the worms would like some water to drink. Big mistake...

The next day, the nice man drove out from town and handed us $75 dollars – pure profit for those five thousand worms (if, like most business people, we didn't count our time). We had barely had the time to show our father our money at dinnertime that night when the phone rang. Apparently worms with water and heat die rather quickly. The worm buyer was understandably angry. But he didn't want the money back; he wanted worms. Doing what was right, the next day we went digging for another 5000 worms. This time it was much harder. All the places we had harvested the worms the day before were pretty much empty. We had to resort to digging around in our mother's garden (knowing very well that we were risking our lives doing that). We found another 5000 worms, but it took a long time, and we wrapped up the worm business shortly after we walked back into the house. **We learned the hard lesson that your product has to be good each and every time you sell it.** We also realized that the worm business was one that we didn't really want to be in and shut our doors.

Every business has times in its lifecycle where it isn't profitable. The fact is that 50% of businesses are never profitable and end up shutting their doors within 3 years of starting. For some businesses, this period of unprofitability is just a short time during start-up; for others, this might happen during an expansion, downturn in the economy, or after there has been a technological shift (VCR to DVD, for example). Even low overhead businesses, such as a sole proprietorship selling a simple product or service, have a period where they have expenses without generating revenue. There are many reasons why businesses aren't profitable which we will get into later. I myself, like many entrepreneurs, have owned a couple businesses that weren't really profitable for periods of their existence.

Winetux

In 1986, I was in my early 20's and started a company that brought a new and innovative product to market called Winetux. This

Stop Your Bleeding

What do you need to do to Stop Your
Bleeding in Your Business?

- Set goals for what you want?

- Fire your worst customers?

- Hire a proper bookkeeper?

- Let a staff member go that is
causing dysfunction?

- Stop thefts?

- Start paying yourself more?

- Fire poorly performing sales team members?

- Hire a new operations manager?

- Get your cash flow under control?

- Get a handle on your accounts receivables?

- Delegate more tasks so you have more free time
to work on your business development?

- Find out where your cash is going?

- Book yourself personal time off so you can rest
and recover?

product used a new technology that would keep a wine bottle cool on your table on a hot day. The design of a tuxedo was supposed to add class to any occasion. Friends loved it. They thought it was going to be the next Rubik's cube. I managed to raise the $10,000 we needed to get the business off the ground from friends and family. I found a designer and contract manufacturer and went on the road selling the product at wine festivals, gift shows, and to retailers. The problem was that while the product concept was a fresh and novel idea, it was not a necessity item. Furthermore, we made the mistake of not doing enough market research. If we had, we would have likely found that many people don't like covering their bottles. In fact, they like showing off the labels.

We hadn't clearly defined who the target market exactly was or determined the best way of selling to them. The One Page Business Plan by Jim Horan wasn't invented in those days, but had we used it, perhaps our vision for the company and the product would have been much clearer. We would have focused on wedding parties and wedding stores where we could see some volume. Perhaps we would have realized that we needed to serve niche marketplaces where covering the bottles was not an issue. In the end, Winetux wasn't profitable because we didn't have the strategy, money, or resources to get the sales we needed to ensure its viability. The whole endeavour resulted in a near physical and mental breakdown for me. Like many small business owners, I was bleeding energy. I was run ragged trying to ensure the operation was successful, and doing all the jobs from managing production contracts to marketing, bookkeeping, and sales, while figuring out how I was going to pay back my shareholders. In the end, there was enough value in the business and the patent that we were able to sell it and was able to recoup enough to pay my shareholders back.

Mother Maria's Market

The second time I almost went broke was in 1999. We had built our first store, Ave Maria, into a successful operation. My business partner Louis, a land developer, had built a strip mall west of town, and we decided to open up a larger, more varied store there. Instead of sticking to our working model, I thought that a concept based on stores I had seen in more metropolitan communities would be even more successful. We leased a location twice the size of the original store in a location with much less traffic and opened Mother Maria's. Not only did it have both organic and regular produce and dry goods, it also boasted a deli, bakery, and coffee shop. My lack of research into the location and the viability of the final product; overconfidence in my abilities; cost overruns; and lack of judgement in hiring and other decisions led to a catastrophic failure. In the first year, we lost $272,000, a fortune for a small business. We were bleeding cash. The store's average sales were much lower than expected. We had fewer customers than was needed to meet expenses. The bank manager was calling almost every day to ask why we were in overdraft. I had to make some tough decisions. I sweated every time we had to make payroll. The cash flow issues were taking a physical and mental toll on me. Finally we were able to secure additional financing that gave us the time we needed to make changes. We eventually turned the store around enough to become profitable, but I now fully understood the stresses related to business failure. In order for your business to be profitable in the future, you need to take control of the issues that are holding you back.

Do It Now! Identify Your Bleeding

Before we go further in our pursuit of making your business more profitable, let's look at your business in an objective fashion. To do this, take a few minutes to identify the threats to your business and to your industry.

Is your business under attack today? What are the threats?

Identify from Whom, How, and Where. Is it from competition? Employee theft? Customers? Pricing? Government regulations? Technology? Something else?

What are the issues causing you to not be as profitable as you need to be? What are your weaknesses or your blind spots? Write down as many as possible. Remember, no one else will do this for you - so be honest.

What do you need to do to stop any bleeding in your business? Are you bleeding money? Are you bleeding customers? Are you bleeding staff? Perhaps you are just bleeding your time? What is the source of bleeding? Can you put a dollar figure on what this is costing you?

What needs to happen to stop that bleeding?

What are you going to do first?

To fight off threats and attacks on your business you need to focus on what you do well. What are the things that you can use not only in your defence, but to go on the offensive? Perhaps you have a great culture in your business? Maybe you have the best sales training and therefore have an advantage over your competition? Perhaps you have a great product or an innovative service? Perhaps you have a faster service or lower cost? **List 10 things that your company does well:**

1.   6.

2.   7.

3.   8.

4.   9.

5.   10.

Issues that Cause Stress for Owners of a Struggling Business.

1. Pressure from financiers and banks to turn the business around.

2. Partner-related issues caused by breakdowns in communications that may have contributed to business failure.

3. Stress caused by lack of clarity about the next steps to take.

4. Mental and physical fatigue that affect the owner's ability to turn the business around.

5. Staff issues may come up as staff feel stress when they see the business struggling and may have insecurities about their own abilities to face potential layoffs.

6. Issues related to lack of skills that owners have that prevent them from making change.

7. The feeling of shame that owners feel internally because of the apparent failure of the business and their inability and weaknesses to make significant change. This leads to lack of confidence and self doubt.

8. Frustration with the time it takes to turn around a floundering business

Use Opportunities To Move Forward With Your Business

What are the opportunities that you have right now in your industry and with your business? List 4.

1.

2.

3.

4.

Now, how can you capitalize on those opportunities if you had all the required resources?

What would it mean for your business?

What would it mean for you personally?

How could you profit from these opportunities?

Having lived those experiences, it is easy for me to see how business owners faced with struggling businesses can turn to destructive behaviours that lead to sad consequences in their personal and family lives. Here are some of the issues that lead to significant stress for owners when their business is struggling.

As a community, we need to provide support and have compassion for those who are struggling in a business that is in trouble. If you are finding yourself in a similar situation with a failing or unsuccessful business, I feel for you. I am committed through this book to help you turn your business around to the point where it is profitable. Hopefully you have enough finances, determination, energy, support, and time to make that happen.

A wise person once said that "**money and profits can't bring you happiness, but a lack of profits and money sure can cause you stress!**" As business owners, we all have our reasons for starting a business: we want to help others, we want the lifestyle of working for ourselves, and we want to make money! Nothing wrong with any of that. The problem is that we seem to be working harder and harder but not getting further ahead. In fact, many business owners get over their head trying to figure out how to run their day-to-day operations and dealing with all the issues that they can't focus on improving their profits. Yet there are some simple ways to increase profitability and lessen stress by focusing on key areas, which we will discuss in depth in this book. First, however, owners need to be aware of a couple areas that are key for a business to run successfully.

I was working with a business owner, and I asked what was stopping him from doubling his sales. He paused and looked at me and said, "No one has ever asked me that question. I am not sure." So if I were to ask you the same question (what is stopping you from doubling your business?), what would you tell me?

Personal factors often hold business owners back

I have worked with numerous business owners who have been held back because they want to ensure that everything is done perfectly. They don't let their staff do what they have hired them to do. This limits the business to the owner's capabilities and the owners end up burned out. Sometimes it's our personal upbringing, self-image, or internal messaging that tells us that we can never be a success. Many times as business owners we should be working on tasks that will allow our business to grow and prosper, but we get caught doing things that are not important or urgent because we are afraid.

7 Things Business Owners Fear

Fear of Failure

Failing in our business after putting in so much time, energy, and money can make us lose face. We have probably been putting on a brave face all the while knowing that things are not always going well. We are afraid of failing our family who have believed in us and of not being able to "bring home the bread." We might be afraid to fail because we will disappoint our employees and even our customers. I even worked with a business owner who was afraid to fail because she would let down the previous owner that sold her the business, for too high of a price I might add!

Fear of Losing Control

Business owners don't want to lose control and as a result end up micromanaging their businesses. "No one can do it as well as I can" is often heard in the small business environment. However, it is exactly this fear of losing control that holds business owners back. Only once you overcome this fear and start delegating tasks can you move your business forward. Successful owners hire people that are better than them and let these people do the job they were hired for.

Fear of Not Knowing What to Do Next

When we own a business, we think we should know everything; however, this is impossible. Often business owners are great at the technical aspects of the business and end up faking the other stuff. Don't be afraid of getting help in areas where you don't have the expertise. In order to know what to do next, often we need to slow down and not rush our decisions, but at the same time refuse to be conquered by inaction. Feeling overwhelmed is often the symptom of not having plans in place and following those plans.

Fear of Success

As strange as it might seem, some business owners I know don't believe that they can be successful and have a fear of success. Sometimes this relates to upbringing and being discouraged or doubted by others. Sometimes owners don't recognize that they are successful and have managed to get to where they are. They are doubtful of taking the business to the next level. By celebrating successes and recognizing what you have done well, along with having goals that are achievable, you can overcome this fear.

Fear of Being Thought of as Crazy

You are stepping out on a limb by taking on a business venture and some people will think that the risk is incredible and that you are crazy for doing it. Pay no heed to the naysayers unless they have experience in what you are doing, but listen closely to good advice. Avoid those with little else left to do than bring down those leaders like yourself who are able to see bigger things! It's the big dreamers like you who turn those dreams into action who make change in the world!

Fear of Thinking Big!

This can be related to some of the other fears, which all can be related to our upbringing or our life's history. However, thinking big can be scary for small business owners, even though it is necessary.

Unless you can think out of the box and try new things you will be forever stuck with small profits and a struggling business. Think and dream big regularly and move your business forward with incremental steps until it grows as big as your dreams! Don't limit your business; make it so you and your business are opportunity seekers!

Lack of Business Knowledge

As a business coach I work with business owners on a regular basis that have not reached their full potential because of self-limiting factors. Sometimes it is simply the lack of knowledge on how to grow their businesses, how to increase sales, or more importantly how to make their business profitable. Often times the business owners don't have sales systems, good marketing practices, or financial systems in place that enable them to be successful. It's hard to measure what you don't understand. If this is holding your business back, take some courses or get someone to help you with this area of your business so that you can become more successful. The fact that you are reading this right now proves that you are committed to increasing your knowledge of business, which will lead to your success.

To truly be successful, business owners like you and me need to determine what is causing us fear, and determine whether that fear is holding us back or pushing us forward. By understanding the drivers and the psychological barriers we might have to our success and working on those, we can truly achieve things thought impossible by others.

I have worked with many highly skilled business owners who are extremely talented at what they do. The problem arises when these business owners become successful as a result of their skill and their business grows. The skills that enabled them to be successful as a small business have been outgrown by their success. This can lead to problems. In every group, there are some entrepreneurs who are blind to their lack of knowledge in areas that could lead to their success. In other words, we have technicians starting a business because they know everything about how to build a product or service but fail to realize that they don't have the knowledge of how to communicate with the customer, price the product, or lead the employees. This is exactly why great businessmen and -women hire people who have the skills, talent, or aptitude to do a job better than the boss. If you are the owner of a company, never be afraid to hire people who are better than you. Once you have hired them, make sure you have HR systems in place that will ensure you have long term stability in your organization.

Do It Now! What Do You Need to Know?

Step 1. Make a list of 5 things that would make a significant difference for your business if you knew how to do them:

1.

2.

3.

4.

5.

Step 2. Pick one item from this list and make a commitment to pick up a book on the topic over the next week.

Time Management, not Micromanagement!

There are only so many things that a business owner can do in a day. It seems like weekly I talk to another business owner who is working 50, 60, 70, or more hours in a week. These people often tell me that if they don't do something, it won't get done. There is a mentality that nobody can do it just like they can or they feel that they need to lead by example and show their staff that they work harder than anyone in the company. The problem with this picture is that, when this happens, owners become burned out. The growing mountain of jobs that need to be done and the never-ending work pile overwhelms them. They feel aggravated when staff ask for time off for holidays or family life because they don't give themselves that time. **Once burnout sets in, entrepreneurs start making decisions that aren't wise. They either fail to hire staff that can bring the proper skills to the job, or their micromanagement overrides decisions that could improve the business.** This lack of leadership paralyzes the business and leads to business failure over time.

If you struggle with micromanaging, you need to develop habits and put systems in place that are going to lead to your long-term success and viability. A system is the order, steps, or process of running your operation so that it is consistent and smooth. By running your business with systems, you will ensure that each and every time something gets done, it will be done to your level of technical specifications. To do this, you need to determine what specific areas and tasks need to be done. This will relieve you of your need to micromanage. **List the tasks that will enable you to stop micromanaging your business. Set a training program for your staff that has a measure of accountability. You will find that, all of a sudden, your 60-hour work week has dropped to 40 or less.** The ultimate goal of a business owner should be to create a business that can run sufficiently without them being in the business on a day-to-day basis. Once this is accomplished, you will create value in your business. This will help to make your business sellable. If your dream is to own a business that makes money for you while you have coffee with your friends, or go on holidays with your family, you need to set systems in place.

To ensure your valuable time is used efficiently, you need to put an end to micromanagement. Here are some ways you as a business owner can reduce your stress levels!

Keys to Time Management:

Document your systems to ensure that the things you need done get done.

Train your staff and have regular reviews to keep them accountable to their job descriptions and operational systems.

Hire better people than yourself. Sometimes business owners are intimidated by people who are better then them. Great leaders draw people around them that have skills that are better than theirs so that they can focus on leadership. Small business owners are leaders. Start acting like one!

Take a holiday. Yes. Get away from your business and take a break! On your return, make a note of what was done and what fires needed to be put out. What is on your desk? These are the thing that you need more systems in place to take care of. This will reduce your need to micromanage in the future.

Make a list of 6-10 things that you need to take care of the next day and do this before the end of the workday or the night before. It has been proven that business owners that make lists are more effective and have less stress.

Prioritize your list, check off your list each day, and avoid getting side-tracked by phone calls, email, social media, and things that are not important. Focus on building and growing your business and the profits will come.

Do It Now!

1. Write down all the things you do in a typical week.

2. Determine which of those things are essential and which you can and will delegate to one of your staff. If you are a

consultant or a one person business, what jobs can you hire someone to do for you?

3.   Make a list of steps that are necessary for this to happen. This might mean writing down the specific tasks involved in doing a certain job to your requirements, picking someone to be a trainer, or setting time to do it yourself.

4.   Set a deadline for when it will happen.

Health Tip for Business Owners: Adrenal Fatigue?

When our businesses are under attack we are running on our adrenals. Adrenal fatigue is characterized by low energy, the inability to sleep, mind-racing and overall restlessness.

Symptoms of adrenal fatigue include:

- lack of concentration

- memory issues, and

- lowered immune systems.

Adrenal fatigue is your body's way of saying no more! Nutritional supplements that nourish adrenal glands (which can get you on the path to recovery) include, licorice root, maca, Siberian ginseng, ashwaganda and B vitamins. There are specific adrenal support products in your local health food store that are formulated to get you sleeping better and increase your energy in a positive way. You don't have to feel exhausted. Get rest and get help.

Final Note: My friend Paul was badly hurt in the bear attack. His friend Dave Trepanier had saved his life. As a group, we made sure he wasn't going to bleed to death. Paul's elbow was shot off and the bear had mauled him extensively. We drove 3 hours down some dark rough roads in the middle of the night to take Paul to the nearest hospital. He was rushed into the operating room and a fantastic medical staff saved his arm. Today he has extensive scarring but has regained some mobility. Paul is lucky to be alive. I am so thankful for all the things that went right that night, despite all that went wrong!

Chapter 3: Slip-Sliding Away - Setting Profit Goals

Why you need to set the stage for your success

The snow in the Rocky Mountains in February can make for the best skiing in the world. At the age of 22, I was loving every minute of a ski trip with my buddies. The sun was warm, the sky was blue, and the temperature was perfect. Skiing on a run aptly named "Hell's Kitchen", in the back bowl of Lake Louise with my friend James (who was a much better skier than me), made for an exhilarating afternoon. Our other companions had taken an easier run to the bottom.

The hard snow crunched under my skis as I gathered up my courage to head down the steep slope. I had only made two turns on the hard pack when I lost my balance and fell backwards. Sliding down the mountain, head first, on my back, and out of control, I car towards the rocks and the cliffs below. As I was pror the danger, I knew instinctively that the collisi was going to seriously end any future skiing enjoy.

my life). I felt desperate. I was grasping for anything that could save me. My adrenaline was rushing and my mind screamed through my available options. In what seemed like a lifetime, but was really a millisecond, I understood what I had to do. I flipped my skies over my head and stood up. The change in direction was immediate. The force of my weight on the skis sent them shooting across the slope away from the danger.

Synopsis: A business in trouble is like skiing out of control. As owners we feel desperate, our adrenaline is often racing, and we grasp for any straw that can help us get out of the danger that is threatening to end the life of our business.

A Business Owner Out of Control

Tanya was also sliding out of control when I was invited by her husband to work with them to get their business back on course. Tanya had been working too many hours. In fact, she and her husband were competing to see who could put the most hours into the business. Tanya was exhausted from working so much. As a result, she felt overwhelmed, under-supported, and unappreciated. The family business was making money but should have been making more. Like many other business owners, her belief was that she had to do everything herself if she wanted the jobs done right. The couple had bought the business from her father-in-law several years before, thinking that they were on the path to financial freedom. Instead, Tanya now felt like she had been sold into slavery. She was unsure that business coaching was going to be anything more than an additional unwelcome cost to her business.

I started working with Tanya and her husband as I do with all clients, with the belief that they know their business better than I ever will. We started off by determining what they wanted out of the business and proceeded to move in that direction. I worked with Tanya to start scheduling her time at work. I challenged her on her need to micromanage the business, and Tanya and her husband started training their staff with systems to make them accountable for their actions. Tanya and her husband set goals for what their business would look like in 1 year, 5 years, and 15 years. They wrote down the steps that would be needed to achieve these goals. This all took time. But what transpired was similar to what happens to a butterfly coming out of a cocoon. The business started to work like businesses should. No longer out of control, Tanya felt less stressed and the business became more profitable. Tanya and her husband started to have a healthier relationship at work and it showed. The key to the change was when Tanya and her husband agreed on what they wanted out of the business and started working towards that vision.

Setting the Stage for Success - How You Can Create A Vision For Your Business and Your Life!

Most business owners I know would like to have more profit and be more successful. After putting so much into their business, they often can't understand why they are not making the money that they think they should be. **According to the National Federation of Independent Business, over the lifetime of any given business, only 39% of businesses are profitable, 30% break even, and 30% lose money, with 1% falling in the "unable to determine" category** (NFIB, 2013). Many research organizations have suggested that the leading cause of business failure is undercapitalization or, in other words, a lack of cash that a business has to get to profitability. My experience with businesses and business owners over the years would suggest that while **businesses do run out of money and are forced to close up, the underlying causes are not lack of cash but lack of vision!** Much of this has to do with the focus of the owners and their outlook on life. Often times, business owners are disappointed because the business isn't successful, but they haven't honestly defined success.

Lack of Clear Vision: Think back to when you started your business. Did you have a plan for where it would be today? Many businesses are started because someone had an idea that they could make a lot of money opening a business. This would mean that they don't have to work for anyone else, can make more money than they would as an employee, and can finally be in control of their future. **The lack of a concrete vision of how this is going to transpire along with a lack of business experience or the skills necessary to ensure success are paramount to the failure of the business being profitable in the long run.** There are a variety of tools that business owners can use to ensure that they create a vision for where they are going. These include things like the One Page Business Plan, working with organizations that help startups, taking business classes, and even getting business colleges or universities that have students eager to work on research projects to help you out. In his book *The E-Myth Revisited*, Michael Gerber suggests that entrepreneurs need to think about what the business is going to be in 5, 10, or 25 years down the road and start building towards that. Fortunately, the road to success and increased profits can be fairly simple, but it takes an intense and focused effort with determination to succeed.

What Does Success Look Like for You?

As the business owner, you need to start by defining what success looks like for you and your business. A simple way to do this is to take time and write it down. Many business owners never do this because they believe that they know what they want and how to get it. **Research and science both show that by writing down your goals, your chance of success is increased significantly.** In an important study by Dr. Gail Mathews of Dominican University, of over 260 business owners and professionals in the United States and worldwide, there was a significant difference in the success rate between people who just stated their goals and those who actually wrote their goals down and provided weekly updates to a friend (Matthews, 2007). In the study, participants were broken down into five separate groups. Each group had to think of business-related goals that they hoped to accomplish over the period of the next month; rate those goals in terms of difficulty, importance, and the resources they had; and then accomplish those goals.

- Group #1 just thought of the business-related goals,

- Group #2 wrote down their goals,

- Group #3 wrote down their goals and their action steps to achieve the goals,

- Group #4 wrote down their goals down and their action steps and sent these commitments to a friend, and

- Group #5 went further than any of the other groups and also sent a weekly progress report to a friend.

What happened next is what typically happens to all business owners when they just think of goals but don't make concrete plans to follow through. **By the end of the four-week study, only 43% of Group #1 had accomplished their goals** or were halfway to completing them. Compare this to the business owners in Group #4 who wrote down their goals, made action steps, and told a friend about them. This group accomplished (or were more than half completed) 64% of their goals. **Finally, if we look at Group #5 who were sharing their goals and giving progress reports to be accountable, we see that a whopping 76% of goals were actually completed or halfway there.** This not only goes to show that writing down goals works but also that being accountable to those goals can make a significant difference. Thus another argument for working with a business coach.

There is some additional science to writing things down with the intention to follow through and many books have been written in this area. For example, Wayne Dyer made himself famous by focusing specifically in this area. The science I am talking about is the reticular activating system (RAF) in your brain. Setting your intent is quite a powerful way of concentrating your brain to ensure that you are able to stay focused on this goal. **Writing down the goals and action steps that accompany that goal can significantly improve your willingness to accomplish your goal and help you focus on getting them done. It is in this way that you trigger your brain to help you follow through on your intentions and have a higher likelihood of success.**

One thing I ask all my clients early on in our relationship is to write down their goals. I am often amazed to hear that many of these successful people have never taken the time to write down what they want to be doing 1 year, 5 years, or 15 years down the road. Like most people, they are floating along in life hoping to get somewhere without realizing where that somewhere is. **The amazing fact is that setting goals or planning doesn't need to take a lot of time. In fact, it's been said that whether you take 3 days or 30 minutes to write down you goals, there will not be a significant difference.** When writing down your goals, it is best to start with what you want your business to look like farther down the road. For example, I usually start by asking my clients to write down what they want in 15 years, then we do the exercise again for 5 years out, and finally down to 1 year. **Start your goals with "I am" or " I have:"**

- I have $50,000 more in the bank.

- I have paid off my line of credit.

- I am going on weekly dates with my wife.

- I am going to the gym 3 days a week.

Smart Goals

To get the best results, we want to make SMART goals: Specific, Measurable, Achievable, Realistic and Timely.

It's no use writing down goals that we know we are never going to achieve. Such goals simply set us up for failure. However, unless we dream a little, we will never have anything to set our sights on and achieve. I coach my clients to set goals in a number of areas, such as physical, spiritual, relationships, financial, and business. Sometimes clients ask if they need to set spiritual goals as they are not religious. I am not saying that you need to do this. However, I believe that there is a difference between spirituality and religion (although some people might not make the distinction). Spiritual factors affect your spirit or a connection to something bigger. For some people, this is religious, and the connection to that religion is important. For others, this can mean sharing what they have with others, spending time meditating, or living in the present moment. I believe that for business owners to be successful, there needs to be a bigger reason for why we are doing this. Once I explain this to clients, there is rarely any further explanation needed. In terms of other goals, some people like to lump business and financial together; however, I tend to feel that goals for your business can be significantly different from your financial goals. Of course, whatever works best for you is what you should do!

Know What You Want – Goal Setting

Grab 3 sheets of paper and a pen, or download the guide sheets from the website www.profityourselfhealthy.com/bookdownloads/. On the top of the first page, write 1 Year; write 5 Year on the second; and write 15 Year on the third. On the body of each page write down these titles: physical health, spiritual goals, knowledge and education, relationship goals, financial goals, and business goals.

Set a timer on your phone, watch, or clock for 2-3 minutes. Start the timer and write down your goals starting with **"I am"** or **"I have,"** keeping in mind the timeframe and how old you will be at that point. Some people prefer to do this in point form, which is fine. Just remember to start each point with "I am" or "I have." This exercise should take a maximum of 10-15 minutes! You will probably have several items under each title. For example, you might write things like:

- Physical Health Goals

    - I am going to the Gym 3x per week

    - I am eating breakfast every morning after my walk

- Spiritual Goals

    - I am spending 10 minutes a day being grateful for things that I have in my life

- Knowledge or Educational Goals

    - I am taking a course to help grow my knowledge of business

- Relationships Goals

    - I am going out for 1 date night a week with my spouse

    - I spend time with _____

- <u>Financial Goals</u>
    - I have $X in the bank
    - We have paid off our _____
- <u>Business Goals</u>
    - Our business has hit X$ in sales
    - We have a marketing manager in place
    - Our sales team...
    - We meet...

Finally, review your 1-Year Plan. Pick one goal that you think is the most important - work on this goal, even if it isn't your business goal. Physical health and relationship goals can be just as important as business goals. Set your timer to 5 minutes. Now write all the things down that need to happen for you to reach that goal.

At this point you can do two things: 1) either share your goals with someone you trust, or 2) fold up your paper and put it away in a drawer somewhere that you will stumble across it in a few months. The first option is preferable because, as the Matthews study showed, you will have greater success if you are accountable! Share it!

Build Your Team for Success!

The best way to achieve your goals is to surround yourself with people to help you along the way. After writing down your goals, you know what you need to do to achieve them, and building a team around you as you grow helps to ensure that you will. Take the time to develop your dream team.

The key to having a great team is creating a culture that fosters the values that you believe your company and you stand for. Writing down these values or doing it with your team gives clarity to your expectations. As the owner, you need to be consistent in your representation of these values. Everyone is looking to you as the leader of the team, and if you do not have the same values and treat your staff with respect, care, and consideration, why should they treat each other that way or your customers, for that matter? Take time to find out what is going on in the lives of your employees and create a safe and happy business environment where they are excited to come each and every day of their working lives. For your employees to function at a high level, they need to have a clear understanding of what is expected of them. This should be in writing with SMART goals and regular reviews of these goals. To be effective as a leader, you need to check in regularly with your management team to ensure that everyone is on the same page and to coach them to higher levels. Monthly staff meetings, training for all your employees, and regular quarterly reviews will all move your company forward towards achieving your goals.

Do It Now!

Here is an organizational Chart for a typical small business. **Put your name beside any job that you do now.**

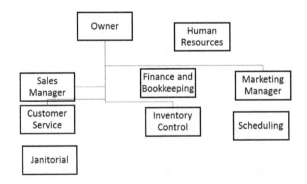

Your Small Business Org Chart

Keys to Happy Employees

- Know the company goals
- Have a clear understanding of what is expected of employees
  - Measurable goals and targets
  - Written job descriptions
  - Training checklist
- Regular reviews
- Quarterly or semi-annual employee reviews with feedback and positive enforcement
- Regularly scheduled salary reviews
- Profit sharing program (if applicable)
- Daily communication and expressed interest in who they are!

Daily: Talk to every staff member (if possible) and touch base with them about their family and any job issues. People tend to work better for people they like than those they don't.

Weekly: Regular manager meetings and coaching sessions - these might not be more than 15 minutes, but they may need to be several hours. Use this time to ensure that your managers are on task and on target with the company goals for that time period.

Monthly: All-staff meetings. You need to have regular meetings to communicate clearly about projects, updates, policies, tactics, and any issues that need to be discussed.

Quarterly: Personal staff reviews to discuss targets, positive things you notice, as well as challenges that the particular employee might be facing.

Health Tip For Business Owners: Relationship Help

If you are working in your business with your spouse, there are times when things are going to get stressful. This stress often has a detrimental effect on business owner's relationships.

One way to defuse this stress and improve your relationship is to get professional marriage counselling. This counselling is confidential and is often covered by your business's insurance programs. If you are paying for it and need it, why not use it? Your marriage will appreciate it and, as studies show, if you are happily married, you will live a longer, healthier life!

Chapter 4: Playing To Win - Getting the Profit Mindset.

How having a strategy can increase

your chances of profitability!

We were travelling at over 60 miles per hour when he hit me from the side. My head slammed against the door and my seatbelt cut into my clothing. The metal of his car grinding against mine rang in my ears and the smoke coming from his wheels as he tried to force me off the pavement burned my eyes. Just when I thought things couldn't get any worse, I was hit by another car at full force on the passenger side of the car, sandwiching me between the two of them. The hood of the car flew up blocking my view. The first driver braked quickly and hit my rear quarter panel. My car spun out of control and I flew towards the light post at the edge of the track... My mind was a blur. This was not the way it was supposed to end!

I had invested over $1000 in the car (which was a lot of money for me in those days). I had, however, made up my mind, weeks before, that I was going to win the race prize money to cover my costs.

I didn't win the Hit To Pass, but I did come second overall. After two days of racing, I took home a huge trophy, a nice cheque that more than covered my expenses, and a bad case of whiplash. My car was a write off, and I wasn't sure how I survived. One thing is certain though: if I hadn't been so determined to win the prize money, I never would have succeeded. I was playing to win!

Synopsis: How determined are you to win this race called business that you have entered? Many small business owners are not focused on the finish line; they are enjoying the atmosphere, the noise, the distractions. You can still enjoy the experience, but the mindset of playing to win is a game changer that can set you apart from other mediocre businesses.

Roland Gahler knows what it takes to create results and has the drive to see it through. In the late 1950s, his father had a small business distributing herbal tinctures and other products made in Switzerland to a few health food stores and delicatessens. As a youth, Roland helped mix and fill bulk herbs and other products by hand. This led to him working in the natural food industry in the early 1970s. Even then, as a young man, he was well aware that the business absolutely needed to change, and the focus had to shift to manufacturing products that were supported by science. Roland developed the first goat's milk acidophilus products over 30 years ago. Now everyone in the industry, including major drug companies, is in the probiotics business. Under Roland's leadership, Factors Group never lagged behind in innovation; if anything, they were ahead of their time.

Roland remembers in the early 1970s when Factors sales were less than $30,000 a month. Now they are an international company that has become one of the largest supplement manufacturers in North America – a direct result of Roland's drive and of "wanting it bad enough" or, in his words, " a lot of blood and guts – no one came and did us any favours."

So what strategies have worked for Roland? To be successful, Roland believes that companies and leaders must be true to their word. **"If you**

say you are going to do something, you have to do it to the best of your ability." Factors was built on the fact that they upheld their commitments, even if, financially, it was not in their favour. To this day, Factors continues to honour their commitment to maintain specific brands for specific markets, even though many others in the industry have dismissed their commitment by saying "it's just business" and fleeing the industry at the sight of more dollars to be made elsewhere.

By building capacity in their production facilities and through smart acquisitions, Factors was able to achieve economies of scale that helped them strengthen their brand by actually lowering costs for their customers. As the business continued to grow, Roland realized that he needed more control over raw materials if he was going to put a truly effective science-based product into consumers' hands. To that end, the company bought thousands of acres of pristine farmland in the Okanagan valley of British Columbia, where it started growing and harvesting its own organic herbs and botanicals. To this day the company continues to spend millions of dollars each year on infrastructure so that it can produce the highest quality products and outperform its competitors.

When I asked Roland what strategies small business owners need to implement to be successful, he replied that success in business starts before an entrepreneur opens a business.

"It's fine to think your mom's secret spaghetti and meatballs recipe is the best and, therefore, you should open a restaurant, but that doesn't mean you'll be hugely successful. Just look around: how many restaurants and small businesses fail each and every year because the owners don't ask enough questions. They place too much focus on their special product or secret ingredient, instead of caring about the consumer and what matters to them."

According to Roland, many business owners aren't flexible. Often, they have policies and procedures that make it difficult and complicated to do business with them. As a result, customers leave. Then, with the business failing, the owners bad-mouth the customers and blame the clients for making poor choices. This is wrong.

Successful business owners think long term. What can I do today to make my business stronger over time? How can I create an experience for my customers that will make them come back? This means hiring the right people to interact with your customers, delivering a product or service that is memorable, and developing relationships with your client base that will last for decades. This creates value. Businesses need to re-think what they are doing to ensure their future success. This may mean working cooperatively with other similar businesses, suppliers, and customers to come up with a framework that creates more value. Are you strong enough to assess your strengths and weaknesses and humbly make the changes necessary to be successful? Think out of the box in ways that will drive new business and create opportunities that you haven't envisioned before (Gahler, 2016).

Strategy in Non-Profits

In 2004, I was the co-founder of a non-profit group called PACHA, which sought to improve air quality in our community. With three pulp mills, an oil refinery, a number of saw mills, and other industry, Prince George had been known as the armpit of British Columbia, if not Canada. The air stunk and Prince George had some of the highest rates of illness in the province. The air was affecting the health of the community.

Our group wanted to make a change but realized that what had been done in the past had not worked. None of the government initiatives or public collaboration with industry was changing the fact that people were getting sick. So we decided on a different approach: our strategy was to change the way that the public related to industry. Our core group of 6-10 people quickly grew to thousands of members. We now had legitimacy.

We decided not to play by the rules, and we discussed issues in the media. To make sure the issues moved forward, we set up our own meetings with government, industry, politicians, and the public. Instead of relying on government and industry to do testing, we did our own. We took letters from children and people made sick by the air and sent them to the CEOs and board members of the polluting companies. The results we achieved as a community, with the help of industry and government, were significant. Within 8 years, we had achieved a 40% reduction in particulate levels and a 60% reduction in odor. Our strategies had worked.

What is your Strategy? Who are you Serving?

Part of the problem that many business owners have is that they are unsure of who they are serving. How many times have you seen a small contractor with the sign saying they service residential, commercial, and industrial customers? As a result, the business lacks the focus it needs to ensure that it is using all its resources to maximize its success. As we see with Natural Factors and PACHA, these two organizations were truly focused on what they saw as their core purpose. They were not bound by the status quo. Many businesses want to focus on doing everything for as many customers as they can; they try to be all things to all people, and fail. **Successful businesses define who they are, what they do, and (more importantly) why they are doing it.** Natural Factors serves traditional health food stores with science-based products because they want to remain true to their word and believe that traditional health food stores can make a difference in the lives of consumers. PACHA was a community-oriented organization that used communication to create change because it believed that people shouldn't be sick because industry was dumping toxins into the air. How focused is your business? What is your strategy?

Strategy refers to how your business goes about achieving its objectives in its particular industry. Natural Factors has a strategy for how it pursues its objectives in the health food industry. This strategy includes how they determine what products to sell, what price points they will use, and how to deal with competition. The strategy also includes how to deal with demands from the mass market for their products, as well as how to ensure that they have quality raw materials to make their products. Currently, Natural Factors is developing a business strategy to ensure that their customers are healthy and vibrant for the long term.

For your business to be successful, you need to develop a strategy that suits you, your lifestyle, and the opportunities facing your business. For this to happen, you need to be focused and clear about where and with whom you want to do business, where the opportunities are that you identified earlier, and how your business is going to grow. I like to use an analogy of going fishing.

Ponds - Where are you going to fish?
Vehicle - How are you going to get there?
Bait - What bait are you going to use?
Net - How are you going to capture profit?

Do It Now!

Define Who You Are and Why You Do it

Before you even go fishing, you need to know why you are going. Typically, people go fishing because they love fish and like spending time outdoors. Some fish to relax and others fish because their friends or family fish and they like spending time with them. In business, we fish for customers so that we can enjoy the profits that those customers bring. But why are you in the business you are in? What gets you up in the morning? What drives you to want to make sure that business works? What do you love about what your business does? In order to get clarity about what your business is really about, you need to define those reasons why you got into business and why you are still there.

Why Do You Do What You Do?

List 10 reasons:

1.	6.
2.	7.
3.	8.
4.	9.
5.	10.

What is the Key Reason?

Ponds - Where Are You Going to Fish?

You have started your business because you believe that there is a market for that business, but sometimes the number of opportunities overwhelms us. **You need to identify the areas where you are going to have the greatest chance of success to make sure your business is profitable.** In other words, we can't fish everywhere. Some ponds only have small fish, but other lakes have huge fish. Sometimes these spots with the big fish may be harder to get to or there may be too many other fishing boats in this area, resulting in too much competition and too few fish. If you want to be really successful, it's important to find the best fishing spots: those with little (or no) competition and big fish! Where are these fish?

For example, if you own a restaurant, you might say that you are going to focus on the families with children and lovers of Italian food who live in a particular geographic area.

These different groups - or fish - may be geographic, or they might be identified by culture, age, industry, distribution channels, market segments, technology, or even price. Are there different product categories you are fishing in? How big are you going to get? Write down as clearly as you can where you want to do business and with whom. Be as specific as possible.

List the fish you are trying to catch:

1.   6.

2.   7.

3.   8.

4.   9.

5.   10.

Of the groups that you have listed above, think about the ones you like working with the most. Which groups do you have customers in already? Which groups do you understand the best? Pick 2 or 3 that you think you should focus on.

1.

2.

3.

Vehicle – How Are You Going to Get There?

When we go fishing, we need to get to the fishing hole. But in business, we need to be clear about how we are going to achieve our goals. How are we going to get to the size we want? How are we going to serve our customers? This can be simple when we are talking about a brick and mortar store that is located in a certain community. However, if you are planning to grow your business to a multi-location, multi-market, or even a multinational enterprise, you need to determine how you are going to do it. What are the things you need to do to grow? Perhaps you are happy with the vehicle you have, but if you are planning to change it, write it down.

For example, one of my clients is planning to grow their business and, in order to grow, they need more space. Their 5-year plan includes adding on to their current location and buying some adjoining property to allow for growth.

Some other vehicles to get you moving include alliances, acquisitions of similar businesses or competition, joint ventures, internal growth, and expansion with the use of technology.

How Will You Grow? What business building techniques are you going to use to get your business to succeed and profit the way you would like it to?

1.

2.

3.

Bait – What Bait Are You Going to Use to Hook Your Customers?

To create and maintain an advantage in the marketplace, we need to differentiate ourselves from the competition. You also need to decide what you want to focus on to ensure long-term viability. Understanding your customers will help you to do this (we will get into this more in the advertising chapter). For now, take the time to identify why your customers are attracted to your business and how you can improve.

Image

Some businesses use image as their bait. Some people (and fish) are attracted to shiny things. Having a great image and reputation can attract many potential customers and keep your existing customers hooked. What can you do to improve or build your image? Are there certain things you can do in the media, online, or through direct communication with your customers that will build your image and reputation? Perhaps you can build your image on great service, or great flavor, super food, or your relationships with your customers.

List 3 things on which you want to build your image and reputation:

1.

2.

3.

Price

Is price going to be your bait? Though it can attract customers, be careful with this bait as you might attract sharks to your fishing grounds. There is always someone who is prepared to offer greater discounts than you can. Also, consider that if you are competing on price, you may be undermining your ability to be profitable. We will discuss pricing in Chapter 11, but if you know how you are using pricing to attract customers, write it down now.

What pricing strategies are you using?

1.

2.

3.

Customization

If you can build custom products or services for your clients you may be a winner. In their book *Custom Nation*, Anthony Flynn and Emily Flynn Vencat describe in detail how providing services in a one-size-fits-all product offering is going by the wayside. One just has to look at the likes of Netflix, Starbucks, or any dating service to see that by customizing products to meet the needs of customers, we can increase profitability and customer loyalty, and generate huge sales. Custom Nation author Anthony Flynn built a business called YouBar by customizing meals and granola bars for his customers (Flynn, 2012).

Are there things that you can customize in your business that will add value to your customers? What are they?

1.

2.

3.

Speed

Some businesses pride themselves on being able to deliver their product to their customers faster than anyone else. FedEx has built a whole business around the speed of their delivery. Perhaps you have similar systems? You might not be in the delivery business, but if you can capitalize on your strengths to get your product to your customers hours, days, weeks, or even years faster than your competition, you might have a winner.

Do you have a speed advantage or disadvantage?

Does speed make a difference to your customers? Why or why not?

What can you do to increase your speed?

Technology

Do you have a technological advantage over your competitors? Earlier in the chapter we talked about Natural Factors. One of their advantages is that they invented new processes and used technology and science where there competitors didn't. As a result, they were able to expand and control market segments, increase profitability, and create higher quality products. Apple has been on the forefront of technology in their marketplace. They are not necessarily the first to use certain technologies, but they understood their customer needs and wants and capitalized on them. Think of your own community.

Is there anyone you can think of who has used technology to create an advantage for themselves and attract more customers?

Is there technology developed (or perhaps not yet developed) that would change how you do things, giving you an advantage?

Perhaps there is technology you need to implement just to catch up. What is that technology?

Net - How Are You Going to Capture Profits?

This is a big question for many companies and a crucial one that you need to be clear about. We are going to start diving into this in detail in the next few chapters, but we need to consider both expenses and revenue when we understand how we are going to capture profits. RyanAir grew into one of the world's largest airlines because it was able to come up with a model for reducing expenses in an industry that is fraught with costs. RyanAir was able to create profit because it was able to fly passengers at costs that were significantly lower than its competitors. Some businesses, like boutiques, use another profit model and, instead, offer premium service and charge premium pricing. Drug companies sell drugs that cost them pennies to make for hundreds of dollars, simply because they have proprietary rights. Some businesses in the manufacturing sector are able to offer the same product to different customers at different prices because they have different needs.

Write down how you capture profits now, realizing that this might change by the end of the book. You might have a variety of ways. Write them all down.

1.   5.

2.   6.

3.   7.

4.   8.

Health Tip for Business Owners: Mental Calmness

As business owners, there are times when we need to be calm. L-Theanine is amazing for this. Clinical studies have demonstrated that L-Theanine reduces stress, improves quality of sleep, diminishes the symptoms of premenstrual syndrome, heightens mental acuity, and reduces negative side effects of caffeine. *Natural Factors Mental Calmness* is an awesome product to help you feel calm. When we are calm we make better business decisions!

Chapter 5: Don't Be Blind To Your Profit Potential

How businesses make money

When I was 6 years old I went blind. Not in a figurative sense, but literally blind. Well, at least I thought I was blind. Let me explain. My brothers and I took turns sleeping on the top bed of the bunk beds in our house. While I was the eldest, Rob and Paul sometimes got the "privilege" of sleeping on the top bunk for a few months of the year. This was one of those times. So there I was sleeping on the bottom bunk; Rob, who was a year and two days younger than me, was sleeping on the top. One morning I woke with a strange feeling. I tried to open my eyes but couldn't. Everything was black. I heard Rob climbing down the ladder and Paul scramble off to the bathroom. As hard as I tried, I couldn't open my eyes. I started to panic. "Mommy, Mommy," I cried out. "I can't see, I'm blind, I'm blind." I heard my mother as she came running from the kitchen followed by my brothers. It seemed my eyes were glued shut, no matter how hard I tried to open them. As I panicked, more my voice reached a feverish pitch. I heard my mother's calming words in my ears. "It's okay David. Robbie, go to the bathroom and get a warm cloth." Rob ran off, his feet pattering against the linoleum as he moved towards the bathroom. He returned shortly and, as he threw the cloth to my mother, I felt the warm water splash on my arm. Mom held the warm cloth to my eyes and, as if by magic, my eyelids separated, and I started to see the first light of morning sun. My panic subsided and I knew it would be all right. "It's only pinkeye," she said with a chuckle, as she left me to change out of my pyjamas. "You get to stay home from school today."

Synopsis: As business owners we are often blind to the opportunity around us. This blindness is apparent when we look back and consider some of the mistakes we made. For you to really succeed, you need to take the blinders off and look for opportunity!

How My Blindness Held Me Back in My Business

I can tell you that there have been times in my business career where it has been my own short-sightedness that held me back. I once went into a health food store in the mid-1990s that was doing triple the business I was doing. I was amazed. The store was smaller than ours, it had fewer products, and yet it was more successful! It spurred me to double my own sales over a period of years.

Sure, I used different tactics, but in reality I had been limited by my perception of what was possible in retail until that point. Another time, a friend of mine, Boyd, called me up and asked me about an investment property he had seen. Even though I cycled past the property every day, I had never seen the sign! We bought the property together and eventually sold it for a nice profit. I had been blind to the potential around me until Boyd alerted me to the possibility.

The next step (and the reason that you have picked up this book) is to make more profits. To do this we need to be very clear about how business works and where we can make the changes necessary to improve profitability. Let's do it!

Clarify Your Vision

**If you have been following along
until now you have:**

- 10 things that you would like to do with your profits.

- A clear plan about what you want from your business and your life over the next few years.

- A list of some things that might be holding you back.

- A list of areas where you could free up more time to work on your business by delegating tasks to others.

- A clear vision of why you have your business.

- An idea of who your customers are.

- An idea of where you are going to do business, and

- An idea of how you are going to grow your business.

It doesn't matter if you have a one-person consulting company or a Fortune 500 corporation, because the principals are the same. Businesses need customers who are willing to buy our product or service and, as the customers buy our products, we turn those customer purchases into profits (after paying our expenses). The total value of the profits depends, however, on what transpires in the business: from marketing strategies to management decisions. To make healthy profits, we need to understand how business works and make changes that maximize our return. The changes do not necessarily need to be substantial, as we will see later. However, focused strategies that improve our business in key areas will result in a substantial improvement to the bottom line. As you go through this book, I will show you exactly how to make those tried-and-tested changes and how your business will improve. I have taken the following slide courtesy of the PBCA to show exactly how these different areas work in a typical business.

How Your Business Works

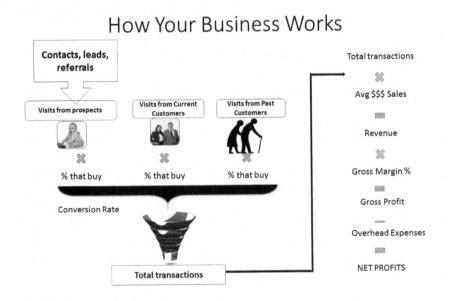

Contacts, Leads and Referrals: All businesses need prospective customers (people that might be interested in our product or service). How we identify and reach these prospects is determined in our marketing plan, which we will go into deeper in the following chapter. In fact, we will go over strategies to help you reach these prospective customers and turn them into paying customers. The key thing here is to understand that prospects are potential customers.

Existing Customers: Unless you are just starting, out all businesses have existing customers. These are the people that are currently buying your product or service. As business owners, sometimes we are so focused on getting new customers that we take our existing customers for granted. Once you have identified what market you want to play in, your existing customers in that market are key to your ongoing success and profitability.

Past Customers: Over time, some of your customers will decide not to buy from you. Some do die off (literally) or perhaps move away. Others choose to buy from your competition, are buying online, or for some reason are not buying from you . As a business owner looking for profits, we need to know why these people are not buying from us, if simply for the fact that we don't want to lose any more customers. Better yet, we want to transform those past customers into buying customers once again.

Conversion Rates: How many prospects have converted into customers? Online companies are great about considering their conversion rates, but how many brick and mortar business owners look at how many customers come through their doors and leave without purchasing? What can we do to improve those rates? What can we do to increase the number of times that our customers buy from us in a given year? There are a number of strategies you can use to improve conversion rates.

Average Sales: What can you do to increase your average sale? You have the customers buying from your business (which is the hard part); now, think about how you can sell them more of what they want. This increase in average sales can make significant differences to your business. I will show you concrete ways and provide ideas that you can use to increase average sales.

Margins: Gross margin is the amount of money that you have left after paying for the cost of the products or services sold. By dividing this number by your total revenue, you get your gross margin percentage (also called gross profit percentage). This is important because this is the profit you have made before your fixed expenses or those expenses you must pay to run the business. Think about areas where you can increase your margins. A 1% margin increase on 1 million dollars is $10,000. Many business owners undervalue what they sell because they don't believe that they are creating value for their customers. By increasing your margins, you will increase your profitability (unless of course you get too greedy and your customers decide to shop elsewhere). We will address all of this in Chapter 10.

Cutting Overhead: Overhead is what you spend on expenses to run your business. This is an area of focus when we get into trouble or when times are tight, but we forget about it when things are good. Are there areas in your business where you can make some cuts in the near future that will affect your bottom line for the year? Probably!

One way of reducing your stress as a business owner is by increasing your profits to the point where you are sufficiently satisfied with the outcome. Of course, being human, we will not ever be fully satisfied with anything in life, and most business owners naturally want more when they achieve a level of success. However, if business owners – Business 2 Consumer and Business 2 Business - improved their performance by 10% in the areas above, they would double their profits! Yes, I did say double! Work on improving each area simply by 10%, and you will double your profits.

As business owners, it is important that we don't try to do it all at once. Instead, we need to focus specific time and energy on each area and try to improve that area incrementally. By measuring your results, you will be able to see what happens, what works, and what doesn't. The key is to understand that incremental changes will lead to significant results over time. As we saw in the previous chart, a business using our formula is easily able to increase their bottom line. Still sceptical? Let's get started and see what we can do to improve your profits.

Do It Now!

Identify 3 areas based on the basic business formula on page 62 that you think you would like to focus on first! Write them down here. This might change as you work through the book, but start here!

Health Tip for Business Owners: Feeling Down?

Maybe you are not getting enough Vitamin D! By getting outside more often and enjoying the sunshine, your mood will improve. In areas where darkness sets in early, try supplementing with Vitamin D or eating foods such as eggs or sardines. Taking time to enjoy the sunshine, even for a few minutes a day can relieve the stress associated with a business and help you feel better naturally.

Chapter 6: Why People Love Babies But Hate Your Advertising

How to reach prospects and turn them into profitable customers

By most accounts, you could say I was a late bloomer. Perhaps I was just slow, but I didn't have my first real girlfriend until I was 23. It's not that I didn't want a girlfriend; I did. I saw lots of prospects but couldn't get anyone to buy what I was selling – me. In those days there was no online dating where you could "advertise yourself." It was all about networking. If I would have known then what I know now I would have changed the way I advertised the fact that I was free. You see, if I would have carried around other people's babies more often, I could have become a chick magnet! People love babies! When you are holding a baby, people come and talk to you. When you are a guy, you will find that most of these people are girls. Perhaps it's because you are not threatening, or perhaps it's because they want what you have. Maybe it's because you have something that is bright, fun, and new! Babies are compelling, interesting, engaging, captivating, and stimulating. They look nice, smell nice (sometimes), and sound nice (sometimes). They are the future success and everyone wants to be part of something successful.

Now I want you to think of your advertising. When you are reaching out to your prospective customers, are you stimulating, interesting, captivating, funny? Do you look great, sound nice, or even smell fantastic? **If you are like most business owners, chances are your advertising more resembles a baby's diaper than it actually does a baby. Let's face it, most of your advertising stinks!** It's more about your company than it is about the customer! When was the last time you looked closely at your advertising or promotions? How are you measuring their success? How much is your advertising costing you for every customer that you have turned from a prospect?

Every successful business has one thing in common: they are able to connect with their customers and provide a product or service that the customer is willing to exchange for money. **Success happens in our customer relationships when we stop focusing on what we have and start focusing on the needs of our customers and filling them.** The more we can learn about our customers and what they want and need, the better off we will be. The web and libraries are filled with books and courses about marketing to potential customers. The problem for business owners is that we become too overwhelmed. We see so many opportunities that our heads are swimming. To be prosperous, we need to know who are customers are and why they are buying from us.

Do It Now! Identify Your Customers

Take a piece of paper and write down 3 things about your **ideal or best customers** or clients. As business owners, sometimes we have customers we don't like dealing with for a variety of reasons and others we just love.

Checklist For Knowing Your Customers

1. Who are they? Make a list.
   a. Name your 10 best customers
   b. Are they in a geographic area?
   c. What age are they?
   d. Are they a business or an individual?
   e. Who makes their buying decisions, and why?
   f. Do they have names and are easily identified?

2. What do they need from you?
   a. Are they buying to fix a pain or to increase pleasure?
   b. Specifically what does your product or service do for them?
   c. What urgent need is it filling?

3. How can you reach them?
   a. What do your best customers have in common?
   b. When and where do they hang out?
   c. What do they like to do, read, or listen to?
   d. What are their interests?
   e. What ages are they?
   f. What do they do for business or a living?
   g. If you were going to send them an offer inviting them to do business with you, what would be the most effective way of getting through to them?

1. **Who are your best customers?** What is it that you like about them? Why do you love doing business with these particular customers?

2. Where are your best and ideal customers coming from now?

3. Why are they buying from you?

4. What are you doing for them to keep them coming back?

Now that you have answered that, think about your prospective customers. Focus on a specific niche in your target market that's made up of your best customers to identify others like them who you haven't reached yet.

The more you write, the clearer it will become. If you can say where your best customers came from, and have clearly defined who they are, the greater chance you have of getting more like them. But you have to be focused!

Advertising to your prospects and customers!

The road to failure is littered with the history of businesses that had great products but, for one reason or another, were unable to convey the value to their prospective customers. Sometimes, business owners think that advertising is an unneeded expense and skip it. As a result, they fail to reach their customers. Many times, businesses pour money down the drain because their advertising is useless. The quicksand of conventional wisdom suggests that you must advertise your business. Advertising sales reps make you think that, by advertising, you will automatically be guaranteed results. In some cases, these owners might be better off putting that money in their pocket giving it away to charity because they don't measure the results! **The problem with most advertising (besides the fact that it doesn't work) is that it is not measured.** In other words, we advertise our product or service and don't even determine if we got customers or sales as a result. We place an ad and we move on.

With great advertising comes great results. The secrets of great advertising include knowing your target market and figuring out the right message that will reach that target market. If you can do that, there is a good chance that your business is going to be successful, and this success will lead to increased profits! If you own a business you need to know a few things:

1. Why should your customers buy from you instead of your competition?

2. What do you do that is special?

3. What is your unique selling proposition?

4. What exactly sets you apart from others in your marketplace?

5. Are you seen as the leader or the follower?

6. Why are your customers buying from you?

7. Is it price or is it your service?

Typically, customers buy because: 1) they have a pain and you have a product that will fix that and decrease that pain, or 2) they would like a pleasure and you have a product or service that will fill that desire or increase that pleasure!

For example, if your business is selling scuba diving trips off the coast of Maui, you are selling to the need for increased pleasure – specifically beauty, nature, relaxation, sports, family outing, or any other reason your customer is buying tickets to your adventure. If, however, one of your clients gets bitten by a shark and needs to see a doctor, the clinic is selling services to fix the pain. This is no different from a sawmill or steel factory whose products are typically sold to customers who will be in pain (financially) if they don't have your product. You might be able to appeal to the purchaser's need for pleasure by creating a fun relationship that is in the interest of both parties to continue.

Pain and Pleasure - Take Your Pen

a. List 5 pains that your industry's product or service (including your competition) alleviates.

1.

2.

3.

4.

5.

b. List 5 pleasures that your industry's product or service increases

1.

2.

3.

4.

5.

c. List 5 things that people don't like about your industry. What are their frustrations? What have you heard complaints about?

1.

2.

3.

4.

5.

Marketing and engaging prospective clients or customers is like a dance. Your partner might not say yes the first time you ask. However, the principles of marketing are simple. If you have correctly identified who you want to target and have figured out the best way to reach them, you have done the bulk of the work. It doesn't matter whether you are advertising on the Internet, social media, radio, television, or in print, the method is essentially the same. The formula that works in advertising that has been proven time and time again.

Your Headline has to Catch Their Attention!

Most ads still fail to produce results even if they are created in the right media at the right time, because they fail to catch the attention of the prospective buyer. This is simply wasted money. For your advertising to be effective, you only have a few seconds to catch the eye of the reader with your headline. In an ever-increasing world of attention-grabbing media, your ad has to stand out, offer a benefit, or promise a result that appeals to the pain or pleasure of your target market. Your headline should not say anything about your business but should focus instead on the intended audience. For this reason, many great ads have the word "you" in them. Perhaps your killer headline addresses something you listed above that consumers hate about your industry. Victor Schwab, an advertising genius from the 20th century, made a list of 100 of the best advertising headlines. Look closely at some of them and notice how they are crafted:

- The Secret of Making People Like You
- A Little Mistake that Cost a Farmer $3000 per Year
- The Last Two Hours are the Longest and Those are the Two Hours you Save
- Why Some Foods Explode in Your Stomach

- Why Some People almost always Make Money in the Stock Market

- When Doctors Feel Rotten, This is What They Do

- Who Ever Heard of a Woman Losing Weight and Enjoying 3 Delicious Meals a Day?

- Discover the Fortune that Lies Hidden in Your Salary

- Is the Life of a Child Worth $1 to You?

- Does Your Child ever Embarrass You?

- For the Woman who is Older than She Looks

- Last Friday, was I Scared...My boss Almost Fired Me!

What did you notice? Do these look like ads that you write?

Use your list and write 5 attention-grabbing headlines for your business or top product or service right now! Make the benefit to the customer eye catching!

1.

2.

3.

4.

5.

Your Body Has to Keep them Engaged!

Your headline has hooked the reader—your prospective client. Now what? Many people can catch your attention with a great one liner but fail to keep you engaged with the details. In the body, tell the reader why you are dramatically different or, in other words, why your product or service is going to make such a big difference to them. In his book *Jump Start Your Business Plan*, Doug Hall says that the key to this part of your ad has to be about giving your audience a "Real Reason to Believe" (Hall, 2001). Some of my best advertising over the past 30 years has worked because I have included testimonials or stories that have given my readers information that is credible and proven. Sometimes it's the guarantee that is all the difference. Here are some things you can do to add credibility to your ads.

- Talk about what is special about your product or service: perhaps ingredients, awards, processes, patents, or licensing.

- A 100% money back guarantee it's almost expected these days, but there is no harm in stating it.

- Guarantee something that your competition doesn't.

- Think about guaranteeing a part of your product or service that is different.

- Give your readers or listeners testimonials to consider; these might come from customers, experts, authors, government, or your staff.

Call to Action

There needs to be a call to action in your advertising. This means that you need to tell your customer what you would like them to do. What is the purpose of your ad? Do you want the reader to buy your product now? Do you want them to go to your website? Do you want them to call for a brochure? Perhaps you want the reader (a prospective customer) to come into your business, cut out the coupon, or come to your meeting? If you don't explicitly tell your prospective customers, they have no idea what you want. Be clear and precise. Many businesses fail to do this and, as a result, the reader is left unsatisfied because they are not sure what to do next. By helping them with this process, you are improving your chances of success.

My Guarantee:

If you do these 3 simple steps, I guarantee that you will get better results than you have been getting to date. Combine this with your knowledge of your target market and you will get results. But make sure you measure the results. How many people took your call to action? What could you do differently next time? What works and what doesn't?

As advertisers, we often get lazy. We forget the basics and let others build our ads for us without a specific direction. We forget who are customers are and where they are and what they need or want. We forget to ask our customers and prospects to do something that will help them and enrich our business. This results in money going out the window! In order for your business to be profitable, you need to ensure that your advertising does its job and drives people to your business.

Do It Now!

Make a plan to review your advertising spending.

1. Where are you advertising and how is it working? What works and what doesn't?

2. How much money are you spending per year on advertising?

3. Does your marketing manager design great ads that work with the key ingredients we stated above?

4. What should you be doing differently now and in the coming year?

Health Tip for Business Owners: Eyes Giving You Problems?

Research shows that salmon, sardines, and the oil that these fish contain is excellent for your dry eyes. Blueberry is another food that is great for the eyes if eaten on a regular basis! If your eyes are bothering you, get them checked out by a professional. Your headache might not be your business, it might just be your eyesight.

Chapter 7: Profiting from the Customers You Already Have

"Personally I am very fond of strawberries and cream, but I have found that for some strange reason, fish prefer worms. So when I went fishing, I didn't think about what I wanted. I thought about what they wanted. I didn't bait the hook with strawberries and cream. Rather, I dangled a worm or grasshopper in front of the fish and said: "Wouldn't you like to have that?" Why not use the same common sense when fishing for people?" - Dale Carnegie, How To Win Friends and Influence People

Two of my earliest customers in the retail health food business, Bernadette and Jack, were in their 70s, though Bernadette looked much older. In fact, as a heavy smoker, Bernadette would get out of the car, come through the door with the help of her husband, and hold onto the front counter. Jack, who was in much better shape, would walk around the store and pick out what they needed. At first, Jack and Bernadette just bought a couple supplements that they couldn't find elsewhere. They were still loyal to the other health food store across town and enjoyed shopping there, but each time they would come in, Vicki, our first staff member, and I, would strike up conversation with them. We asked them about their children, where they met, and what they were doing that day. As our relationship grew, Jack and Bernadette began to trust us more. When we suggested that they try FLW, quite an expensive supplement used for circulation, they hesitated, but it was clear that Bernadette needed something for her health. She tried the product and committed to the 5-month regime. As the months went on, Bernadette would come in and walk further and further throughout the store. By the end of the five months, she was moving up and down the aisles with ease and energy. They stopped shopping at the competition and came almost daily for years to buy and support our growing business.

Synopsis: As business owners, we need to build relationships with our customer to really discover what they need and solve their problems. How many businesses do you know that don't take the time to build relationships with their customers?

Building Business Relationships in the Trades

Troy was stuck in his business as a tradesman plumber. He came to see me because he said he was tired of scraping the bottom of the barrel. At one time, Troy had a plumbing business with many employees and huge revenue, but as a result of poor business choices and a recession, he lost it all. The toll was heavy; Troy's confidence, customers, and business had hit bottom. Fishing on the internet sites for repair jobs, Troy was working on small jobs for little money and was having trouble making ends meet. We talked about this and, more importantly, what Troy wanted from his business and his future. Troy told me that he would like to have a business with recurring revenue, where he didn't have to find new customers on a regular basis. He had some bigger customers in the past, but admitted that he hadn't put the required effort into building those relationships. We developed his strategy to rebuild the relationships with past customers that he had enjoyed working with. We also worked on his idea of recurring revenue through service contracts. It took only a few months and Troy managed to triple his monthly income and his bottom line. His business took off and his confidence soared. Wouldn't you like to do that with your business?

Courting New Customers or Staying With the Ones that Brought Us Here?

How many of us are so caught up in growing our business and courting new customers that we forget where our bread is buttered. Think about it right now: who is supporting you? What are you doing to ensure that these customers are happy and continue to come back? When was the last time you asked them if they are enjoying your relationship? When was the last time you thanked and appreciated them?

Many companies that have outside sales use a Customer Relationship Management (CRM) system. Often sales teams use these CRMs extensively when they are recruiting new customers but forget them once the customer has been landed. **The key to profitable business is to ensure that your customers are extremely satisfied with what you are providing them. This means that you need to be in regular contact with them. This also means that the relationship must go two ways.** We can't just expect that our customers will continue to buy from us just because we are advertising to them. We need to engage our customers and listen. **Listening to our customers can take a variety of forms but it is a critical step in building a profitable business.**

So What Do We Want to Know About Our Customers?

In his classic book, *How to Win Friends and Influence People*, Dale Carnegie says, "You can make more friends in two months by becoming interested in other people than you can in two years by trying to get other people interested in you" (Carnegie, 1936). If we exchange the word in that phrase from people to customers, there would not be much difference. So when we are talking to our customers, we want to know everything we can about them. Who are they? What brought them to your business? Where are they from? How many kids do they have? What do they like doing? What are they interested in? But, before we start trying to build long-term relationships with our customers, we need to understand why we are doing it.

How Much is Your Customer Worth?

Many people have tried to calculate the value of each customer. Using an economic formula, we can estimate the potential value of the customer. If we want to consider the lifetime value of each customer by thinking this way, we need to take some factors into consideration.

Depending on your industry, churn rate, average annual customer purchases, and margin will all be different. However, you should get the idea that, even though the customer might be making you $100 profit this year, over the lifetime relationship with that customer, the value and the profit they end up putting in your pocket can be significant! This is the very reason why we, as business owners, need to focus on keeping our customers happy.

What Do You Need to Do to Retain Customers and Reduce your Churn or Attrition?

Wow Them

Treat your customers like gold and they will reward you by purchasing your goods and services and giving that gold back to you. There are many great books you can read or seminars you can attend to

> (Average Annual Revenue per Customer x Net Profit%) ÷ Annual Churn Rate (customer turn over)
>
> Let's assume our average customer buys $1000 in products from us per year.
>
> If we calculate our **profit** margin to be 10% ($100 profit per customer per year) and we lose 5 % of our customers per year (churn rate), then:
>
> ($1000 x 10% ÷ 5% = $2000)
>
> The Customer Value in <u>Profit Dollars</u> would be $2000.00 for each customer.

learn about customer service, but really it's all about treating them how you would like to be treated and then going a little further. This means that you need to hire great staff and train them to treat your customers just the way you would like to be treated. In Chapter 9, we will discuss implementing sales models that uncover your customer's needs and describe in detail how you can fill them. I love going into a business where they know my name, and my wife loves going into the coffee shop where they have her coffee ready before she even orders it. Think about it – you love that special attention, and so do your customers. How can you wow them?

Invite Them Back Regularly

If you have a database to track what your customers are buying and how their purchases are changing over time, this can be extremely valuable to you. Use this information wisely to build rapport and trust with your customers and invite them to special sales or targeted offers suited just to their needs. One of the things we implemented in our stores was the use of our database to uncover who our best customers were. It can take some effort, but it really works. James, our IT guy, implemented a program where we could print out names and addresses of these people, and we then sent them gift cards to thank them based on their past purchases. The response was over-whelming. We had new people coming into the store and asking if they could get into our customer loyalty program because they wanted to be rewarded by a store that sent their customers rewards!

Engage Them On A Regular Basis

Communicating regularly with your customers through email, social media, and other means reduces the chance of your competition poaching them. I know of one business that regularly offers free training seminars to their customers and their staff. This adds value in the mind of the customer. Sometimes the information offers suggestions on how to use their product; at other times, it is information related to how the customer can improve their own business. Giving your customers something for free tells them that you value them and that you are interested in more than just money. This breeds loyalty and gives you more opportunity to discover how you can serve your customers better and find solutions to their needs.

Make It Easy For Them To Buy From You

Is there anything in your business model that makes it difficult for your customer to buy from you? Are you open at the right hours? Do you have the right locations, speak the right language, and deal in the right currency? Do you use the best delivery method? What else can you do that will encourage your customers to buy more frequently? Does your competition do anything better than you that has the potential to draw your customers away? Can you add that to your business model? Can you improve on that advantage so that you gain the upper hand?

Do It Now!

Make a list of 3 things you can do to wow your customers!

1.

2.

3.

What Are 3 ways you could invite your customers back more frequently?

1.

2.

3.

What are 3 ways you think your company could engage with your customers more over the next 3 months?

1.

2.

3.

What 2 things could you add that would make it easier for your customers to buy from you?

1.

2.

Why People May Not Like Your Business!

Why Businesses Lose Customers and What You Need to Do About It

It's a fact that customers leave us for a variety of reasons that are out of our control: some die off, others move away, and typically there is nothing we can do about that. However, some customers leave for reasons that are within our control. There are ways you can prevent customer loss.

Number 1 Priority

Sometimes we forget that our customers are the reason why we are in business. We get too focused on our plans for expansion, changes, and profits (among other things), causing our relationships with our customers to flounder. Customers know when they are not appreciated and tend not to shop with us. **What to do about it?** We need to ensure that our staff are continually focused on adding value for our current customers and treating them like royalty. If you have a database, you need to check it regularly to see who has stopped buying from you and follow up. Maybe our customer has gone out of business and no longer needs our product; perhaps it's another reason, but if we don't ask we will never know. Some of the greatest businesses have had their best ideas from dissatisfied customers. Will you be one of them, or will you let your customers just drift away?

Inconsistencies

The first time a customer engages with us sets a lasting impression. If we wow them with great service the first time they come, and do something different the next time, we are inconsistent. If our service from one sales staff is different from another (because of our failure to implement systems that work), we have a problem. Every time your staff communicates with your customer, it should have the same tone and manner that you have taught them. If there are differences in the delivery of the service model or product, you have a problem. **What to do about it?** You need to develop systems that reflect what you expect in terms of the approach to each of your customers. You need to be consistent in the training of those systems with each and every employee, so they know what is expected and the consequence for underperforming.

High Pressure Sales

I remember one year, the day before Christmas, I received a phone call from a sales rep from one of our key suppliers.

"Hi Dave, how are you doing?"

"Merry Christmas, Jim. What's up?"

"Dave, I am just calling you to tell you that you need to spend another $3000 before the end of the week."

"Why is that, Jim?"

"Well, sales have been slow and the sales manager is on my case. I have to get my sales up. I need you put in an order today. You just haven't bought enough from us this year."

At this point the call went from bad to worse and, after a heated exchange, I hung up on Jim. Needless to say, I didn't place the order and I made it a point of dropping our purchases by 25% the following year as a result of this poor customer experience. Jim eventually apologized for the call, and I realized what incredible stress he had been under, but that was beside the point. The point is that we could have easily stopped buying from them all together, and I would have felt justified.

Have you ever bought something and felt pressured? What kind of taste did that leave in your mouth? What were the chances that you would buy from that individual or even the business that person represented? Unlikely, right? **What to do about it**? If you are putting pressure on your sales staff to get sales under any condition, you might have a problem with your sales model. Any company that encourages their staff to be dishonest, or has staff that replicates dishonesty that they see in you, is in trouble. You are bound to lose customers that you will never regain.

High Staff Turnover

Consistency in business is essential. You need your customer to be able to count on you, and you need to know that the money you have invested in your staff training is going to be put to good use. Your customers build relationships with your staff, so having a high turnover is frustrating to your customers and costly to you. **What to do about it**? Having a hiring system that results in great staff for your company is essential. Training these staff and providing them with a safe environment where they feel adequately challenged and fairly compensated can mean all the difference between you having customers for a long period of time or those same customers drifting off to your competition. Lost customers = Lost profits!

Do It Now!

If you can, find out how you can contact some of the customers who have not bought from you for a period of time. This may be 6 weeks, 6 months, 1 year, or longer depending on your sales cycles. Survey them to find out the reasons why they are not buying from you. Write down 4 questions you could ask them that would help you figure out why you are losing customers.

1.

2.

3.

4.

If you could use your database to send out an offer to customers who have not bought from you for a period of time, what kind of offer would you give that would be an incentive for them to come back? List 3.

1.

2.

3.

Health Tip for Business Owners: High Blood Pressure?

Business owners often forget to eat properly because they are so consumed with the business. Snacking on vegetables and fruit instead of processed foods can make a huge difference to your waistline and overall health. For example, celery is great for business owners who have heart issues because it helps lower blood pressure. Walking or daily exercise will also reduce blood pressure. Chances are, if you reduce your stress, your blood pressure will go down; another reason why you need profits!

Chapter 8: Increasing Conversion Rates for Greater Profit

Turning prospects into customers and getting

them to support your bottom line.

Hitchhiking is all about conversion rates. The goal is to get prospective rides to stop, and convert doubters into friends so they will take you for free to where you want to go. No, there is usually no money involved (unless some nice German lady pays for your ticket that you got for hitchhiking on the Autobahn). I estimate that on my forays in Europe, Australia, and Canada, I have hitchhiked 10,000 km (or about 6,000 miles). To convert drivers into stoppers, I would always be nicely groomed and be holding a cardboard sign with my destination and a Canadian Flag. I think it was the flag and the smile that got people to stop; though, in some places it took me upwards of 17 hours to get someone to pick me up. Once in the car, I felt it was my obligation to try to build a relationship with the driver so that I could not only get as far as they were going, but also make it interesting for them. This worked well for me. Often times the drivers would buy me a meal and sometimes they would even take me to their homes and offer me a bed to sleep in. If I was lucky, they would know a friend or another truck driver who was going further in the direction that I was and set me up with another ride.

Synopsis: As entrepreneurs, we are constantly trying to convert our prospects into customers. Perhaps we are not hitching rides, but we are using similar techniques to get people to buy more frequently. It takes a lot of work to convert lookers into buyers, but when you use the right techniques, the rewards can be substantial.

Troubling Times

Ann needed help. Her family business was in trouble. She had started the recreation boat business with her husband because he thought it would be fun. Running the business was fun...at first. Her husband, Bill, had the gift of gab, and they went to shows and sold boats throughout the region. But then things started to go wrong. Bill found another woman and, as part of the divorce proceedings, Ann was left with the business while her husband got the real estate holdings. Clearly, Ann was left holding the bag. The business was in the tank, Ann didn't even want to own it, and her husband was still doing service work for her (even though he caused problems with her customers). She had few sales, and one of her options was to sell the business, but its only value was clearly its inventory. Ann decided to push on. With the help of her supplier, she started marketing to her customer base (many of whom had moved on to other vendors). Ann is still toiling with her business, but getting it to the point where she can sell it for something more than inventory is slowly becoming a reality. She fired her ex-husband, found a new service contractor who is building her reputation, and the marketing is starting to pay off. Her customers are coming back and, when they come through her doors, Ann knows how to ensure her customers leave with what they need. Her sales are going up and she is starting to believe in herself and her abilities as a businesswoman.

When we think about conversion rates, most people think about web-based businesses. **The conversion rate is the actual number of people that buy from your business after having contact with it.** For example, if you get 100 visitors on your website and 1 sale, you would have a 1% conversion rate. In a retail store, you might have 300 people come through the door in a given day and maybe 200 transactions; this would mean that you have a 66% conversion rate. In a B2B operation, you might have contacted 500 customers in a month but only have 100 actual customers buying from you; this is a 20% conversion rate.

Why is your conversion rate important? Think about how much effort you have put into reaching prospects and converting them into customers. Businesses spend thousands upon thousands of dollars getting people to come into contact with them. We do this through advertising, promotions, publicity, referral requests, direct marketing, websites ... you get the picture. **The more of these prospective customers and visitors that you convert into sales, the higher your conversion rate. This will translate into higher sales and higher profits.** Now, we are not talking here about higher *average* sales (we will discuss how you can increase average sales to increase profits in the next chapter). What we are talking about here is your sales model. How are you engaging customers and encouraging them to actually buy from you, and do it more often? To engage our customers more often, we need to first find out why we might be turning them away!

What do potential customers not like about you? Almost every business owner I talk to wants to get more profitable by increasing sales, but few actually ask the question, "Why don't people buy from us?" What is it that people don't like about your industry? For example, if you have a medical supply or health-related business, people might think that you are expensive, have limited stock, or don't have enough educated staff. If you have a grocery store, maybe people don't like the fact that you don't have service staff, are out of stock, or you have poor parking. You may be thinking right now that your industry doesn't have those problems because you sell used cars. Well, let me tell you something you won't believe: people don't trust used car salespeople! If you have a medical or dental office, you need to know that most people hate coming to see you because they are scared! Every industry has reasons why people don't buy from them. What are yours?

What are you doing that frustrates your customers? Is it the long lines? The fact that your sales staff talk but don't listen? Perhaps your product leaks, or has other technical issues? Maybe your software always needs upgrades? Perhaps when your customer gets a product upgrade, it doesn't work properly? Think about the complaints your business has received. Ask your staff or even your friends. Ask your customers!

If you want to increase your conversion rates, you need to figure out **the core reasons that people don't like your industry.** Uncovering this dislike for your industry or your business can be like finding gold. **By overcoming your customer's dislike of your business or industry, you can show prospective customers that they can trust you. You will increase the number of people that will buy from you. You will increase your profits. In short, you will be more successful.** Of course, you first need to identify the problem, fix it, and communicate that to your customer. Once you do, you will be able to convert more prospects, and get your current and past customers to buy from you more frequently. This will save you money and make you profits.

Do It Now!

List 10 reasons why people don't like your business and your industry.

1.

2.

3.

4.

5.

6.

7.

8.

9.

10.

How many of the above problem areas are you already addressing? What are you doing to convey the fact that you are addressing these concerns to your customers and prospective customers? If you fixed any or all of those issues, would your conversion rate increase? Probably.

Some Changes You Can Make to Increase your Conversion Rates

To increase our conversion rates, sometimes we need to make some changes. This can mean physical changes (as you will see) but, more often, it is changes in how we treat our customers and how we relate to them.

Building Trust With Your Customers

Customers don't buy from businesses or people they don't like or trust. To improve your sales to potential customers and to get customers to come back more often, you need to build this trust.

Show Your Customers You Care: Show your customers that you care about them. You need to find out what interests them, what is real to them, what they love, and what they like and hate. As my friend Dennis likes to say, *"God gave you two ears and one mouth for a reason."* **You need to be listening to your customers twice as much as you talk to them.** When they trust you care for them, and really want to help solve their problems, you are well on your road to increasing your conversion rate. If you take the time to really be present with your customers, it won't matter what you are selling, your customers will try to find reasons to buy it from you.

Don't Promise Things That You Can't Deliver: When we first started our store, we built the business by bringing in products that no one else had; specially ordering many of them for our customers. When customers would ask us when a product would be in, I would always say that it was ordered, and it would be two weeks. However, as the business got busier, I couldn't keep up with all the ordering. As a result, I had to change how we promised products. I also realized that honesty was the only policy and that if I made mistakes ordering products, I had to be honest with my customers about that. Again, don't promise what you can't deliver.

Fix The Problem: If you create a problem, or your customer experiences a problem with your product or service, you need to fix it. I always love the story about how the founder of Wal-Mart, Sam Walton, replaced the tires for an old lady who said the wrong tires were put on her car. Walton replaced the tires even though he knew fully well that the tires weren't even bought at his store. **And 50 years later we are still talking about this story. Think about how solving the problem created goodwill.** Standing behind your product and solving problems for your customers goes a long way in building trust.

Never Misrepresent Your Product Or Service: If your product or service can't do something, don't say it can! Sometimes our customers want us or our products to be able to do something and want to buy it to solve their problem. If it can't do what they want, don't sell it to them. You will only look bad in the long run. Being upfront and honest will build trust with your customers and increase your conversion rates overtime.

Stand Behind Your Sales Force: If your sales force has built a relationship with your customer, you need to be respectful of that relationship. If you are hard on your sales staff and they leave the business, or your compensation package is weak and you are always changing sales reps, your customers will become frustrated. Giving your sales reps the tools they need to service your customers over the long run will result in increased profits.

Do It Now!

List 5 ways you could build trust with your customers:

1.

2.

3.

4.

5.

Boost Your Credibility

Customers want to buy from businesses that will sell them products that they can trust. To build long-term relationships with your customers, they want to know that they will be able to rely on you when they need you. Some great ways to build credibility with your customers include:

Testimonials

Using testimonials boosts credibility and can really boost a business, when used appropriately. You need to ask for testimonials. If you have developed great relationships with your customers, they will probably be more than happy to say a few words that you can put on your website, advertising, or promotional material. This makes new customers more likely to feel they can trust you.

Be the expert

One way of boosting your credibility is by touting yourself or your business as an expert. If you have knowledge, write blogs, newspaper articles, and press releases. Offer a seminar and provide staff to be interviewed in trade magazines, on the radio, or on TV. Chances are, you know a lot about something; otherwise, you probably wouldn't be in business. Setting yourself and your business up as the expert can go a long ways to boosting your credibility.

Endorsements

Everyone likes to know that they are buying a great product that is going to make them look good in the eyes of others. Certain types of customers like to buy products that are endorsed by people bigger than themselves. This is why the big brands use big names to sell products. Nike used Michael Jordan to sell basketball shoes because, if the shoes were good enough for one of the best players of all time, they will be good enough for me! Air Jordan's made millions for Nike, and for Michael, because of the credibility. You probably don't have the funds necessary to have Michael Jordan endorse your business, but how about the local mayor, councillor, local actor, or sports star? Even your best customer!

Do It Now!

List 5 ways that you could build your credibility.

1.

2.

3.

4.

5.

Reduce Customer Risk

One of the underlying factors why people don't buy from you is that they perceive a risk. Perhaps they are unsure of the brand, the new product, or your service offering. They want to know that what they buy for their company or their family will leave them in good standing. Identify the risk and offset that risk by communicating value and offering the best warranty. Domino's built a brand on delivering pizza in 30 minutes or it's free. Typically, customers have 4 types of risk perceptions: financial, social, functional, and safety. By building a relationship with your customers and asking the right questions, you can figure out what type of risk they perceive and allay these fears.

Financial Risk: Customers worry that the cost of the product or service you offer will not be equal to the value. You can reduce this risk and create a perception of value in the product by having payment plans and guarantees.

Social Risk: No one wants to be humiliated or embarrassed. If the thought of buying your product has the potential of causing a social risk your customers will steer away. You can reduce this risk by positioning your product to the correct market and engaging with your customers in a way that reinforces their ego.

Functional Risk: Simply put, your product needs to do what it says. Warranties and guarantees can reduce functional risk to your customer.

Safety Risk: If your product has the potential to hurt someone, you need to be aware of that risk and have plans and strategies in place to reduce the risk to your customers. This may include government inspections, certifications, or safety standards that give your customer the satisfaction that you have done everything necessary to reduce the risk of harm to them and those around them.

Do It Now!

What are 5 ways you could reduce risk to your customers?

1.

2.

3.

4.

5.

Increase Conversion Rates with Facility Design and Layout

Let's look at some of the things that you can use to improve your customer's experience and drive your sales and profits up once they are in your business location! As long as you have customers who are physically coming into your business, you can do more to increase conversion rates and sales to these customers by considering some of the following.

Location

Whether you own a showroom, retail space, hair salon, amusement park, lumber yard, or even a website, how you lay out your business can play a big part in how many people buy from you and how often. Location! Location! Location! Even though the Internet has made location somewhat less important for some businesses, for a business based in a physical building, location is everything. For many businesses, geographic location can mean the difference between success and failure. From firsthand experience, I can tell you that one of my retail businesses started with a great idea in a wrong location and failed. If you have a restaurant or a business with retail space, geography is critical to success. Sometimes locating a business properly in a busy area can be all the difference between success and failure. I have experienced businesses that are successful, despite their poor service and quality of product, simply because they have a great location. Other businesses have wasted away because of the owner's failure to situate their business in a high-traffic area in their target market.

There is a science to location. When businesses grow to a certain size, they often start using scientific data for foot traffic, customer counts, and demographics to choose the proper location. If you are considering moving your business to increase traffic flow, you might want to use some sophisticated tools for looking at the demographics of your target market. One choice of some businesses is to be located as near as possible to their most successful competitor. This strategy should be considered carefully (you competitor might out-compete you!), but it can make the difference for some business owners. Alternatively, you may wish to use a blue ocean strategy and consider opening where there is little or no competition. In this case, you need to think about the reasons that there is no competition and add that to your decision-making process.

Your Customers Experience

Once you attract customers, you need to ensure that they enjoy their experience at your business. This can mean the difference between success and failure for you. We have talked about the need for a sales system and adequate training for your staff to ensure that your customers are greeted and welcomed into your establishment. But, as business owners, we sometimes forget to consider how our establishment looks. We often enter through back doors, or rush in to turn alarms off, and never consider things through the eyes of our customers. When your customers come into your business, they need time to adjust. This is typically called a decompression zone. This is an area where they are able to take notice of what is happening: colors and smells. Finding ways of making prospects and customers feel more comfortable in the decompression zone will increase the number that buy from you and your average sale.

Layout for Better Sales

Grocery stores and websites are laid out in a certain way to ensure that you, the customer, spend as much as possible. For example, have you noticed that dairy and meat are usually always at the back of the grocery store while produce and flowers are at the front? There are reasons for all this. Certain areas of your business are going to be able to generate more sales because your customers are more likely to stop and then buy. Research shows that customers tend to move in certain directions when they come in your door. Mapping out where your customers naturally travel and looking when they are in the business can help you increase sales. In North America, most customers naturally turn right when they come into a business. Laying out your product accordingly can draw customers to your displays and make all the difference for your business.

Pick Your Colors Carefully

Certain colors can make your customers buy or walk away. There is research to show that some colors are calming, while others are exciting. Depending on your business, you want to use calming primary colors in many areas of your business and other colors to cause excitement in areas where you want to drive attention. You will also want to use different colors depending on the client base, age, and culture.

Eye Level, Buy Level

Your customers will buy what they can see. If you want them to buy certain products because you make more margin or profits, put these items at eye level. Also, be considerate of who your customers are. There is a reason why grocery stores put cereals for kids on lower shelves - so kids can see them!

Stack Them High and Watch Them Fly

I learned this technique from Danny Wells at a seminar 20 years ago and, as a result, was able to boost sales by incredible amounts in retail locations. By buying product on sale from your supplier or asking for product at a reduced price with a "guaranteed sale," you can stack product up and increase demand with your signage. There has been plenty of research to show that customers who see case stacks are more likely to pick product from them. The mentality is: if there is a huge stack, there must be huge demand and a great price and, therefore, I need to buy it. These promotional sales can sell 4 to 5 times _more_ than regular sales for this product or service over a similar period (Chevalier, 2012)!

More Facings = More Sales

Research shows that by doubling the facing of product in your establishment, you can increase your sales by 30% on the same product. Many products get missed when they are only single faced. Increasing the chance that customers will view the product increases the amount of sales (Chevalier, 2012).

Big Sells More

Research shows that if you are manufacturing, retailing, or selling online, BIG sells! Bigger pictures, bigger product, and bigger displays will sell you more product!

There are countless ways of encouraging and increasing sales once prospective customers are in your location. If you need help, find out what others in your industry are doing. By asking what works at trade shows, conventions, or from your others in your trade association, you can go a long way to increasing profitability. Don't be afraid to ask the experts or those who have been successful in your industry for advice. Chances are, they would be more than happy to share their tips and secrets!

Do It Now!

List 3 specific ways that you could increase your customer conversion rates.

1.

2.

3.

Measuring and Plugging Conversion Leaks

There is no business that I know of that has a 100% conversion rate. Websites with a 2 or 3% conversion rate are typically very successful. The normal rate is often less than 1%. Even destination retail stores have conversion rates that are well below 100%. **What does your conversion rate look like? How many people are contacting you and not buying?** Tracking conversion rates on websites is easy, because there are numerous tracking devices which measure and report to you on a regular basis. However, for small business owners, conversion rates can be a mystery. When I started tracking conversion rates in my stores, I was surprised by a number of things. Firstly, the conversion rate was higher than expected. Secondly, the fact that we were tracking conversion rates really got my staff more involved in ensuring that everyone that came through the doors was taken care of.

How do we track the conversion rate? In our stores, for certain periods of time, we have a pen and paper out in order to keep track of how many people leave the building without a purchase. Often times, the staff make notes of what area the customers are in and what they are looking at; especially if we don't have that product in stock. This is incredibly valuable information because we can plug those conversion leaks. If we have customers leaving because we are continually short of a certain item, we can make sure that that product is in stock. Also, in some businesses, there are times in the day, week, month, or year when there are not enough staff on the schedule, which can result in a loss of customers. Are your traffic counts up but sales down? If this is happening to your business, try to figure out a way that you can plug that leak. Maybe you have certain sales staff on your floor who don't complete the sales? Are your staff doing things at certain times in the day that is preventing your customers from getting served? Do your potential customers act in a certain way at a certain time? Are there more browsers in the evening but fewer sales? Increase sales results and you will increase profit. Measuring your conversion rates is a simple way of figuring out how to get more people buying from you.

Do It Now!

1. Make a point to go through the front door of your business and view things through the eyes of your customers. Start in the parking lot. What do you notice? Is your signage eye-catching or does it just get in the way? Is the grass cut and are the plants trimmed? Once

inside, does it look clean? How does it smell? Do you need new paint? How is the layout? Did anyone greet you?

2. Have someone make the changes you need to improve your business to make it more appealing to the customers.

3. How can you measure your conversion leaks?

4. What are 2 ways you are going to try and encourage more sales with your prospects and customers at your location?

Health Tip For Business Owners: Get More Sleep

Getting enough sleep is crucial for business people dealing with stress on a regular basis. Not only will you have more energy, but sleep also slows the effects of aging. Drop some lavender oil on your light bulbs or in your bathwater to help you relax and get a better sleep! There are many natural supplements that can help you get better sleep. On the other hand, sleeping drugs can increase the risk of early death! Beware!

Chapter 9: How to Sell More To Your Existing Customers!

What you need to sell more with less effort!

In January 1996, Vere was my favorite sales rep. He knew how to develop relationships that would last for ages and transcend mistakes. When Vere heard that I was visiting Vancouver, he suggested that we take some time off and go for an afternoon of kayaking where we could bond and talk business. We had covered quite a distance in the hour or so that we paddled out from the marina where launched. As we glided by the houses and cottages that dotted the shoreline, I thought for a second that we were in paradise. Just then a boat sped by, and I was caught by surprise by the sheer size of the waves. My kayak flipped over. If you have ever been submerged in a kayak in the Pacific Ocean in January, you know three things: firstly, the water is freezing cold; secondly, you are held under the water by the kayak skirt, which protects you from the spray of your paddles; thirdly, you need to breathe. Trying not to panic, I rolled my body up for a badly needed breath. I could hear Vere shouting something to me about pulling the skirt as I went back under. A couple tries later

I extracted myself from the kayak and started swimming to shore, where someone had spotted us in trouble. They came to the rescue with a blanket to fend off the hypothermia that was now setting in. I slowly regained my body temperature, lucky to be alive. Vere was lucky too. It is, after all, hard to explain a dead customer.

Synopsis: Like many great sales reps, Vere knew the value of relationships and how to build them. If we want to build our business, we need to hire people who are even better than us at building relationships with our customers and serving their needs.

A salesman who built businesses based on selling techniques

Dennis Bonagara built and grew businesses based on super sales techniques and great relationships with his customers, but he didn't start out as a sales expert. In fact, Dennis is proof that great salespeople are taught and not born. Of course, there are certain characteristics that make some people better at sales than others, but Dennis's education was in science and math, not marketing and business! Times were tough in 1977 and the first job he got was programming for a software company for $9700 per year! By 1981, Dennis was making $30k per year as a programmer, but was at the top of the ladder, while other company employees had expensive suits and fancy cars. Being a lover of cars and a man of fashion, Dennis asked his boss how he could get into that crowd. It turned out that the senior sales team members were making more money than the programmers.

Taking a 50% pay cut, Dennis joined the sales team. After stumbling around the department without much guidance, Dennis picked up some books on how to sell. He took a Xerox sales course and learned how to build relationships and ask the right questions to uncover people's problems. Dennis found out who was making the decisions related to the purchase of his products and did everything he could to move the sale along. Dennis was good at sales. He was so good, in fact, that they made him sales manager and director of sales. When he eventually left the company, sales had grown from 1 million dollars to 17 million dollars. Not satisfied with working for someone else, Dennis bought into a software company owned by two brothers. When he joined in May the company was tracking sales of $165,000 per year. Just 7 months later at the end of December, sales stood at a rocking $800,000. A few years later, when he was bought out by the brothers, sales were 13 million dollars per year. Finally, before Dennis quit the corporate world to work for himself as a Certified Professional Business Coach, he worked with another company as a consultant and helped build the sales from $600k to 2.5 million dollars in just 18 months!

Unlike Dennis, my first experience with sales was in high school selling chocolate bars door-to-door as a fundraiser for a school club. I wasn't much interested in the club but more interested in the prizes that would be given to the top sellers, so I hit the pavement. Each day after school I would knock on doors and sell chocolates to whomever would buy them. It took determination, persistence, keeping the goal of winning the prizes in mind, and the competition between two others and myself (who outsold the rest of the whole school combined) that made for my sales success. Now, without any formal sales training, I realize I have spent my life in sales of one form or another. Whether it was selling advertising, Winetux products, books, recreational services, houses, investments, vitamins, gifts, cleaner air and water, or coaching services, it has all been sales. Proper training in sales can go a long way to ensuring your business is successful. You can pick up any sales book or take any given sales course and reap the benefits of the training. You'll have increased sales and happier customers. The reality is that sales is a science and not an art.

According to Dennis Bonagara, the key to building huge business sales in a short period of time is having a great sales model that is able to uncover the needs of the customer. **If you don't understand the needs of the customer how can you present a solution to them?** Sales techniques can be learned, and one of the reasons many businesses fail is because they have not mastered the sales model and are unable to fulfill their customer's needs. According to Dennis, **a major reason that business owners get into trouble is that they think they have built the best mousetrap and customers will simply flock to them to buy it. That is not reality!** No one just buys stuff. There needs to be a concrete sales model based on what the product does, its advantages, and what value it brings to the market place.

As a business coach, I often work with owners who have been successful but now feel like they are slipping backwards. If this is you, **one of the key solutions to turning your business back around is by stopping and thinking of all the things that brought you to the level of success you have today!** What has worked in the past? What was the sales model that got your business to this point? Has that changed, or has the business environment changed to the point where it is no longer effective? **Chances are, you just forgot your reasons for success, and once you re-focus, you will be successful.** Additionally, if you start thinking about other markets where your sales techniques could also be effective, you will get results again.

Your Staff and Sales

I like to think that there are two types of sales staff: those who know they are in sales and love the process, and those who are in sales but don't want to think they are. The second type of person is usually in a service-based industry, such as retail, hospitality, or food. However, because of the perception of sales reps, these staff might not want to be associated with sales. **The reality is that every one of your staff needs to understand that they are in sales, just as you are if you are the owner of any business. Each and every business needs to sell something to stay in business.** Sometimes, if you have customers banging down your door, you might tend to forget the need for developing the selling skills necessary to ensure your long-term success. If you are fortunate enough to have a great location, unique product, or a commodity that is always in demand, you might get a certain amount of sales just by being lucky. However, developing a proper sales system for your staff can ensure your long-term profitability and increase the value of your business. Furthermore, training your staff in sales or customer service leads to happier customers, more loyal customers, and prevents the loss of customers to your competitors. Training in sales leads to more profits!

Hiring Sales Staff

Sometimes in business, we need someone to fill a spot, and we pick the first candidate that comes along. This is a terrible approach and one of the reasons that businesses struggle. Without a proper sales system and a systemized approach to hiring the right people, we are setting ourselves up for years of hardship. **As a sales manager, Dennis Bonagara had a rigorous approach to picking sales staff. It was this approach and training that enabled him to build companies from hundreds of thousands of dollars in annual sales to tens of millions.** The biggest problem in selecting candidates is that 95% of people that are in sales don't have a clue how to sell. They don't have formalized training and don't follow a sales model. Good companies take time in hiring. Dennis would always do a behavioural analysis, such as a DISC Behavioural assessment, to find candidates that had the qualities necessary to succeed in sales. Once a candidate has passed through your assessment, you need to ask questions that reveal the true nature and desires of the possible employee.

At this point, you are looking for consistency and continuity of the answers. How do they think, and how does this thinking fit with your company culture? Are there any red flags in their answers? In the sales interview, you always want to ask the candidate to sell you something. Part way through that sale, throw in a serious objection. How do they handle it?

Questions to Ask your Sales Applicants

- What is it that makes you successful as a salesperson?

- Take me through what your sales process looks like?

- When do you stop pursuing a prospect?

- Have you ever turned a customer away?

- What motivates you?

- Have you ever had a losing streak? How did you turn it around?

- What are some of your favourite questions to ask a prospect?

- Tell me about decisions that you made in the past that have brought you to this point.

- Tell me about your childhood.

Great salespeople (the kind that can build your company), are usually interested in sales because of the compensation. Let's face it: sales is a tough job, and there are not many people that really love doing it. Facing possible rejection and stress, day-in and day-out, while trying to close the deal is difficult. Sales people are like mercenaries; they are doing it for the money. If you can manage and compensate the great ones, they will build your company in ways that you might never have thought possible.

Building Profits through Sales Training and Systems

Sales training provides education that can bring your sales force to the next level.

More Sales: By increasing our sales with proven techniques, we have more money to pay our fixed cost, and therefore, have an easier chance of being profitable. Most businesses I know want to sell more of what they have. Having a trained sales force that is backed by great marketing can generate increased sales.

Less Procrastination: A trained sales force has a plan. This plan will lead to less procrastination that's driven by the fear of rejection. No one likes to be rejected but, if your team is properly trained, they will know what to expect and, in turn, know what to do to ensure long-term success. A plan will allow you to get more work done and have greater chances of success with your team. If your sales force has plans in place that enable them to continue to call on prospects even after they have been rejected 4, 5, 6, or 7 times, they will have success where many of your competitors won't.

How to build profits through sales training and systems

Sales training provides education that can bring your sales force to the next level.

Higher Average Sales: Whether you are selling a service or hard goods, in retail or business-to-business, having a trained team of employees who know the fundamentals of sales will ensure that your average sales are higher. This is because your employees will be able to recognize the needs of your customers and service them better. With this in mind, your staff will be able to upsell, cross-sell your customers, and outsell your competition.

Better Communication: Selling is directly related to listening. If you spend money on teaching your employees how to listen, you will benefit from the rewards of that throughout your business. Better communication starts with better listening and better listening results in higher sales.

More Loyal Customers: In an earlier chapter, we talked about the lifetime value of a customer. By employing trained staff that are in tune with the needs and wants of your customers, you are more likely to ensure that your customers are going to be loyal to your business for the long run. Using proven sales techniques ensures that your employees know how to treat your customers which will give them fewer (or no) reasons to buy elsewhere.

Do It Now!

Is your sales team working well for you?

Are there areas that they could do a better job?

How many more sales do you think you could generate with some changes in your sales team or process?

What things do you need to know about sales that would make your company more successful?

Sale Techniques That Work!

There is no end to the number of sales training courses and programs that you can take for yourself and your staff to improve your success rates. However, the fundamental key is to communicate to your prospect that you offer far more value than you are asking them to part with. Before you can even start down this road, you need to know the key strengths and weakness of your product or service compared to the competition. You want to be able to understand why people buy your product. If you can do this on a regular basis, you will have increased sales. Let's break down the selling model.

Build Trust: People are more likely to buy from people that they like, know, and trust. By starting a conversation with your prospect about their life, what they are doing, or things and people they like, they will begin to like you. The funny thing is that, even though people might not know you, if you can talk about things that are important to them and demonstrate a sincere interest, they begin to trust you. Asking open-ended questions to understand their thinking and their problems will go a long way in building trust. Again, this comes down to finding out who you are dealing with and how they are going to respond down the road in the sales process. Making mental notes of how certain customers communicate and behave will allow you to present to them in the manner that best suits them.

Find the Purpose: Whether you are selling a meal, a pair of jeans, or a car, you are going to get some browsers (people who are shopping with no intent of buying), and others who are in a rush to buy. Asking questions that reveal why and when your customer will buy (or not) can determine how much time you need to spend with them.

- "What brings you here today?"

- "Did you find what you are looking for?"

- "What is your timeframe for buying a car?"

It is also good to tell your prospect why you are there: "I am here to help you when you are ready!" "What is going on today that is making you look for a new solution?"

Find the Underlying Cause: Once we have developed rapport with a prospect, we must find out more information about why they are interested in buying. Why does this person need what we have? Is it a *pain* that they want to alleviate or do they want to increase *pleasure*? We need to determine the value of what they need. For example, if we are selling a photocopier to a business, we need to understand the uses for the copier and how badly they need it. Do they need it because the last utility copier broke or because they want to upgrade to something that will make better color copies? Can we determine a financial cost? Are they losing money because they don't have what we sell? How much? Maybe your travel company is selling a trip to Hawaii. What do customers dream will happen when they buy that trip? What does that mean to their family? Their relationships? Once you develop trust with a customer, asking deeper questions can get you better results.

Know the Budget: Don't be afraid to ask about a customer's budget. You might be wasting your potential profit by selling something too cheaply or lose the sale by pitching something that is beyond the customer's price limit. Ask your prospective customer about other systems they have looked at or who they have already talked to. This can give you a good idea of how much they are willing to spend.

Decision Process: Many times, when you have a customer right in front of you saying that they want to buy, you can easily close the deal. However, with more complex products or services, there is usually a longer decision process. It is important to ask who makes the decision and what additional information they need to make a final decision. Sometimes, depending on your type of business, you might have to pitch to a variety of people in a company to get to the final decision maker. You need to understand the decision process of your customer. Ask questions like: "You are probably the most important person in the company that is making this buying decision, but who else needs to be involved and what is the best way to approach them?" Ultimately, you want to get the whole group of decision makers in one room at the same time when you make your presentation.

Present the Solution: Once you know the needs and wants of your customers and have the product that you believe will satisfy them, you need to present your product to the customer. Sometimes, this will be as simple as putting the product into a customer's hand. Other times, you might have to get the customer to make a choice between several potential solutions to their problem. When you have presented the solution and they have agreed that this solution will work for them, then this is the time where you ask for the sale by taking them to the till, writing up the order, and closing the deal.

Follow up: We often forget that we need to have regular communication with our customers to ensure that they are truly satisfied. Using systems to ensure our staff follow up with our customers and clients, enables you to get feedback about the customer experience. We can tweak the system and make it better by using this information. We also want to find out how satisfied customers are with the process and the product to ensure long-term relationships. If they are satisfied with your sales process, this can be a great time to ask for referrals. If the product is fantastic, they may give you leads that will develop into more business by telling their friends about you! After all, word-of-mouth is the best advertising.

Whether you have an inside sales or customer service team, or an outside B2B sales force, if they aren't producing the results, perhaps you should invest in training. Staff training in sales can range from a few hundred dollars to many thousands of dollars depending on the training type and level of training needed. However, the payback for your company can be significant. High quality sales training can let you quickly move your business to the next level. A couple of great programs that specialize in sales training are Sandler Training (www.sandler.com) and SPIN Sales Training. Dennis Bonagara is also a great resource for companies that are looking for coaching and sales training to go to the next level. Dennis can be reached at www.pbstrategies.com or by phone at 201-425-8300.

The sale process for small business owners

Start by Building Trust. People like to do business with people they Know, Like and Trust!

What is their purpose? What does success mean to them?

Find out why they buy? Is it Pain or Pleasure? Uncovering the cost of them not solving the problem can make all the difference

Money What is their Budget?

What is the Decision process? Who needs to be consulted to make the decision

Present the solution. And Ask for the Sale. This shouldn't be done until you know that you have the right solution to solve their painful problem and you are working with the right decision makers

Follow up to ensure they are happy with the product and they could recommend you to others.

- What does your current sales model look like?

- If you had a new sales model, what would it look like?

- What are the weaknesses of your sales team?

- Why do you lose sales to competitors?

- What needs to be fixed in your sales model that will ensure you move your company to a more profitable position?

- Who is your best salesperson? Why?

- Why don't you have more salespeople that are even better than the ones you have now?

- Are you keeping underperforming salespeople? Why?

- What do you need to do to sell more of what you have?

Health Tip for Owners: Have Ulcers? Try Licorice

Some business owners have ulcers from their stress levels and poor food choices. Foods such as coffee, liquor, hot peppers, deep fried foods, and carbonated drinks can cause ulcers or make them worse. Foods that heal the stomach include rosemary, blueberries, garlic, cranberry and olives. Deglycerized Licorice (DGL), mastic gum, and honey have all been shown in clinical studies to heal ulcers of the mouth and the stomach!

Chapter 10: How to Increase Your Margins Without Falling Off Your Bike

Why margins are important and ways you can increase them

Fewer than 48 hours into our honeymoon in Kelowna, Margaret and I decided to ride down to the winery from our B&B. The road down was narrow and busy with traffic but, being the near-pro mountain biker that I was (in my mind), it would be a piece of cake. However, the sheer amount of traffic made Margaret nervous. On the way down the hill, Margaret had to ride off the shoulder of the road and into the gully below to avoid being hit by a vehicle from behind. Flying down the embankment, she landed hard, crashing and falling off her bike. I screeched my bike to a halt and ran back to my new bride. All the cars on both sides of the road stopped to see if she was okay. Margaret was scraped up, but not bleeding. As she was in shock, we hitched a ride back to the B&B from one of the gentlemen in a pickup truck that had stopped to help. Once back, I quickly ran up to our room and grabbed the Arnica Montana (a homeopathic remedy that I had in my suitcase). This immediately helped her come out of shock and as I saw her pupils come back to normal, I realized that the winery tour was out of the question for that day!

Synopsis: Balancing your business pricing and margins is a tough business. Lean too far one way with margins that are too low, and your business could be in the ditch. Greedily lean too far the other way, and you might get caught in the traffic of customers rushing to leave your business. Getting your margins right can ensure that you can have money to take trips to the winery or other places that you dream of going with your family.

A Bike Business

David Lee of Cycle Logic started his bike business out of his garage, like many fledgling entrepreneurs. He saw a need for fixing bikes and was just the man to do it. His business grew because of his attention to detail, quality service, and his ability to relate to his customers. In fact, it grew so big that he needed to move his business a couple of times to accommodate the growing demand for his services and the bikes and gear that he sold. But David made a mistake that is common to many business owners. He was so intent on growing sales that he forgot about his margin. David had grown his inventory and increased his staffing levels, so his expenses had gone through the roof with his new locations. What David didn't realize was that his sales weren't covering all his expenditures. Like many business owners, David was only looking at his financial statements once a year at tax time.

In 2003, David almost went broke. Bad buying habits and overspending had consumed his capital. His debt had piled up, and he had too many staff (some of them at a greater cost than they were making in sales—partly due to poor management). David made some key strategic changes. He reduced his staffing costs by laying off some employees. He diversified his product offering to products with which he could make more money. He chose to do business with a smaller group of select suppliers who offered him exclusive lines, giving his customers more reason to be loyal to him. David also changed his buying patterns so that he could make higher margins by buying at the right time, and he adjusted his prices on other products. As a result of his hard work, margins went up, he paid down his debt, and turned the business into a profit center. David was one of the lucky ones. Through hard work and dedication, he was able to turn a dysfunctional business into a functional business that worked for him and his lifestyle.

My Experience with Margins

It took me a few years in business to realize the importance of margins. Like David Lee, in my early days, I concentrated on sales. In fact, when I came across a sign somewhere that said "Double Your Sales", I took that sign and placed it over the office door so that anytime my staff or I went into the office we were forced to look at it. If you are not a believer in the power of suggestion, try putting a sign like that up for a few years. My business grew and doubled more than once before someone cleaning the office took down the worn and faded sign. Even though my sales had doubled, and even quadrupled, my profit was still just okay. After my run in with the George S. May analyst, which I described in an earlier chapter, I was determined to get my profit up. I focused on margins for a whole year. I changed my margins for different products in different areas of business and even asked other retailers in the industry what they were making. I concentrated on getting better discounts from my suppliers. The result was a margin increase of 6 percentage points over two years. I now had a business that was putting profit dollars in my business partner's pocket and in my pocket.

Sales or Margins?

Typically, we want to concentrate on growing our sales to increase our bottom line. The problem with a purely sales-focused growth model is that we need to fully consider the cost of new customers. How much does it cost to get new customers? How will the increase in business affect our current levels of staffing? Can our location handle more customers? We also need to consider whether or not we are more profitable with more customers. In other words, if our gross profit margin is too low or our expenses too high, every sale is costing us more than we actually make.

Let's put it more plainly. Our goal is to increase sales by $100,000 next year by focusing on getting more customers. Let's assume that promotions to get those customers cost us $10,000. Because of the increase in customers we need to add another staff member – let's say that we end up paying $36,000 a year for that. Our cost of the new business is now $46,000. If our gross margin is 35%, this means that we bring in net $35,000. Therefore the cost of our new business is in effect losing us money.

Sales	$100,000
Cost of Goods Sold	65,000
Gross Profit	35,000
Less advertising	10,000
Increased Labor	36,000
Profit or Loss	(-11,000)

As business owners intent on growing our business, we put so much energy in the growth of sales that we forget that if we tweak our business slightly, we may not need to work as hard to get better results. As my friend Deane Parkes so rightly said in his article, **If business owners increased their margin by 1% on $1 million in sales, this would mean another $10,000 in their pocket** (Parkes, 2016). So how do we do this? Well, that is the $10,000 question, isn't it?

Many business owners and their staff get mixed up with mark-up and margin. To put it simply, a mark-up is the difference between the purchase price and our selling cost. For example, if we buy a product from our supplier at $100 and we sell it at 165% of cost, it will be $165.00. In this case, the **mark-up** is 65%

Margin is the difference between our selling price and our mark-up value as a percentage. In the example above, our gross profit amount ($65) divided by our selling price ($165) gives us a **margin** of 39%. So, in other words, the margin is the percentage of our selling price that is profit.

Mark-up and margin can cause problems in pricing because we think we are getting more money when we talk in mark-up. Additionally, if we try to price our product or service using margin we can run into difficulties, as it is easier to multiply than to divide for most people. Therefore, **I advocate pricing using mark-up but understanding what you are doing in terms of margin.** This means that once you determine what profit you need (let say it's 50% margin), you would tell your staff to price your offering with a multiple of 2 or 100%.

Mark-up Vs. Margin

Cost	Mark-up %	Selling Price	Margin %
100	25	125	20
100	50	150	33
100	75	175	43
100	100	200	50
100	200	300	66
100	300	400	75

To increase our margins, we need to increase the difference between what we are selling a product for and the actual cost of that product. There are two ways to do this: 1) reduce our actual cost of the products we sell, or 2) increase the price we are selling it for. But how do we determine the best margins? One way is to use benchmarking. What you are doing here is looking at similar businesses to yours in your industry to see how you compare.

Below is a list of industries and their average Gross Margin Percentage. Please remember that the margin is the average for all their products or services as a whole and not their individual mark-ups on specific product offerings. Also, services and some product manufacturing gross margin will include labour costs attributed to that product or service. In retail and wholesale type businesses, labour is typically separate.

Industry	Cost of Sales %	Gross Margin %
Accommodations	11.13	88.87
Accounting Tax services	39.89	60.11
Advertising Services	30.03	69.97
Agricultural	43.77	56.23
Amusement	22.04	77.96
Appliance dealer	67.50	32.50
Automotive repair	59.60	40.40
Automotive parts	62.47	37.53
Banking	8.7	91.30
Bars and Nightclubs	32.68	67.32
Beauty Shop	44.90	55.10
Beer Distributor	75	25
Beverage Manufacture	42.91	57.09
Blinds for windows	56.1	43.9
Body Shop	60.52	39.48

Boat Dealer	73.9	26.10
Bottled Water Delivery	56.38	43.62
Bridal Shop	59.46	40.54
Broadcasting	19.21	80.79
Building Construction	77.18	22.82
Car Dealers	85.60	14.48
Carpet Sales	63.71	36.29
Child Daycare	58.40	41.60
Church	33.57	66.43
Clothing Manufacture	61.58	38.42
Clothing Stores	51.54	48.46
Computer Design	28.09	71.91
Convenience Store	70	30
Dental	50.7	49.30
Education	13.44	86.56
Electronic store	69.24	30.76
Engineering Construction	70.01	29.99
Engineering Services	40.06	59.92
Entertainment	14.59	85.41
Equipment Manufacture	68.02	31.98
Fast Food Restaurant	40.5	59.50
Fencing	73.02	26.98
Fitness Facility	37.46	62.54
Food Services	37.70	62.30
Food Beverage Store	71.68	28.32
Forestry Logging	61.89	38.11
Funeral Home	42	58.00
Furniture Store	66	44
Gas Station	88.22	11.78

General Stores	69.33	30.67
Golf Course	23.20	76.80
Grocery Store	80	20
Hardware Store	63.66	36.34
Healthcare	8.70	91.30
Home Store	57.11	42.98
Home Builders	76.80	23.20
Home Furnishings	61.60	38.40
Hospital	56.30	43.70
Insurance	29.29	70.71
Internet Service Provider	10.12	89.98
Jewellery Store	50	50
Language School	47.8	52.2
Lawn Garden	59.70	40.30
Law Office	42.50	57.50
Liquor Store	74.70	25.30
Locksmith	65.97	44.09
Mattress Sales	59.45	40.55
Mobile Home Dealer	75.30	24.70
Motorcycle Dealer	76.91	23.09
Moving Business	63.58	36.42
Musical Instrument store	59.00	41.00
Nursing Care Facility	65.40	34.60
Office Machine Rental	40.56	59.44
Oil Gas Extraction	44.24	55.76
Outdoor Rec	56.72	43.28
Painting	68.70	31.30
Pawn Shop	48.03	51.97
Pest Control	35.59	64.41

Pharmacy	76.40	23.60
Power Generation	56.75	43.25
Publishing	22.96	77.04
Real estate broker	53.64	46.36
Renting Leasing	19.68	80.32
Rental Store	40.77	59.23
Research Development	36.30	63.70
Restaurant independent	41.42	58.58
Roofing Siding	69.52	30.48
Shoe Store	59.89	40.11
Spa Hot Tub	61.47	38.53
Staffing Services	13.49	86.51
Storage Units	46.16	53.84
Swimming Pool Const.	64.27	35.37
Tire Shops	62.61	37.39
Trade Contractors	65.86	34.14
Transportation	31.94	68.06
Travel Services	35.57	64.42
TV &Audio	24.75	75.25
Utilities	28.81	71.19
Veterinary Service	39.60	60.40
Vocation	38.85	61.15
Waste Management	39.17	60.83
Water Purification	61.43	38.57
Wholesale Trade	77.30	22.70
Wood Manufacturing	70.92	29.08

Sources Butler Consultants Industry Statistics February 2016
paulweyland.com/gross_profit_margins.pdf

1. **Buy Better:** Do you have a staff member who is great at details? One who loves to understand when and how to buy products when they are on sale? This might just be your ticket to increased margins. If you don't have such an employee, perhaps it is time to find one.

2. **Benchmark:** Above, we listed a number of industries and their margins. Comparing your company margins to theirs is called benchmarking. You can also ask your trade association or non-competing similar businesses what margins you should be making. By working to hit or beat these targets, you can make a big difference to your profits.

3. **Cash Discounts:** Some suppliers sell products at a reduced rate for cash. If you can get an extra 2% off for paying within 10 days or a similar arrangement, get your cash flow working to take advantage of these discounts.

4. **Exclusive Lines:** Exclusive or private label lines can give you extra margin because you have fewer or no competitors with whom your customers can price check. If you are working on getting more profit in your pocket, start looking for areas of your business where you don't have to compete on price.

5. **Negotiate Better Discounts:** Industry discounts often vary from supplier to supplier and customer to customer. You might surprise yourself. Try asking for better pricing from every one of your suppliers. The chances are that some of them will give you better pricing just because you asked. If you can give reasons why you deserve this better pricing such as your loyalty, years of service, purchasing volume, location, product placement, or even your great looks, you are more likely to get results.

6. **Seasonal Buying**: Some industries offer seasonal pricing if you place an order early or buy products at the end of the season. If this works for you, and you don't mind tying up your cash in inventory, you can make some great margins.

7. **Reduce Direct Costs Associated With Your Product or Service:** Sometimes direct costs are labour costs directly related to your service. Examine ways that you can reduce your manufacturing or service-producing costs.

8. **Repurpose Your Product or Service:** If you can figure out ways of offering the same product or service to a new niche market with fewer inputs, you are improving your margin. Assume that you will have no R&D expenses or expenses related to building that product or service prototype. This will increase margins.

9. **Pricing Properly**: Pricing your product properly is the key to improving margins, and we are going to talk about this in depth in the next chapter.

10. **Just Say No:** If your business is one where you need to bid or can choose to work on low value jobs, and you don't really need the work, take a pass. Low margin work can distract you from focusing on areas of your business where you will make a lot more money.

11. **Increase Sales:** If you have the opportunity to sell one more product or repurpose something you have developed for another market, you can reduce margin and increase profit.

12. **Reduce Theft:** Every business model should include the risk of theft. This theft may be intellectual property, hard goods, inputs, or time. If you can systemize your business in such a way that you reduce the risk of theft, you can increase your margins and your profits.

13. **Inventory Systems**: If you are in the manufacturing industry or in a business where you need to carry high levels of inventory, you can reduce your carrying costs by using inventory systems for just-in-time delivery. This means that you don't have to be borrowing money to purchase product, thus reducing your cost of capital and your inventory costs.

14. **Cutting out Errors**: Many businesses have benefited by sophisticated systems like Six Sigma, ISO 9000, Business Process Reengineering (BPR), or Lean systems. All of these are aimed at reducing errors and costs associated with manufacturing products or services. The main point of these processes is that, through the elimination of errors, companies can gain a cost advantage over their competitors.

15. **Watch the Consumables**: Every business has products that they use in preparation of their product or service. Some businesses, like repair shops and construction sites, have consumables that they use on a regular basis that can be billed to a job. Trackable consumables must be factored as a cost of production or billed to the job. This is the only way to ensure that you are getting paid accurately.

16. **Freight costs**: Freight costs are often one of those costs that are not accurately calculated and included in the cost of the products you are selling. Sometimes freight costs are a significant percentage of your product's purchase price. Ensure that you are accounting for these costs when determining the pricing of your products. Alternatively, reducing these costs can save you margin dollars.

Do It Now!

What is your current gross margin?

Look for the industry most similar to yours and compare it to your current margins. What is the difference? Is there room for improvement?

Which suppliers can you negotiate better pricing with right away?

List 3 ways you think could improve your margin

1.

2.

3.

Which one are you going to work on first?

How much would your profits increase if you increased your margin by 3 per cent (multiply your total sales by .03)?

Health Tip For Business Owners: Biking Works to Reduce Stress!

Exercising on a regular basis is a fantastic way to reduce stress and increase energy. Whether you are going on a bike trip with David Lee to Columbia or walking around the block, make sure you exercise regularly to better your focus and get more done in less time!

Chapter 11: Optimal Pricing for Optimal Profit

The Village of Fort St. James was once the capital of British Columbia, but today is a small village with a scattering of stores that service the First Nations Communities and workers in the mining and forest industries that surround the community. In the early 1990's, I would go up there in the weeks before Christmas with a treasure trove of gifts to sell from tables that I set up on the sidewalk outside of one of the grocery stores. Not unlike the fur traders who worked the area 200 years before, I would trade blankets, lamps, knives, and beads that would be used as Christmas gifts in exchange for cash. I would haggle with the buyers and price my wares in bundles to maximize sales. My sister Marie was often my companion on these trips and, as the dark and cold settled in, we would look forward to a warm dinner with the Kearns family at Camp Morice. As we were closing up that particular Friday afternoon, I was caught by surprise when one fellow, around 30 years old and smelling of a day at the local bar, grabbed one of the hunting knives for sale on the table and held it to my throat. "Give me yer money," he said. I was shocked. I tried to move away but was blocked by the table and his friends. I tried to think of something to say, spewing out "Tabasla," one of the only local First Nations words I remembered from my high-school days. He looked at me wide-eyed. "What did you say?"

"Yay haw Tabasla," I repeated, not knowing what the words meant. He slammed the knife down on the table, chuckled, and motioned to his friends. Together, they staggered away into the cold darkness.

Synopsis: Selling goods in the markets can be rewarding if you are selling things other than knives. There is something to be said for the excitement of doing the deal, and haggling with customers. As business owners, we often get so caught up in pricing our products a certain way that we forget that we have many options. This chapter will outline some of your options for pricing so that you don't cut your own throat!

How You Can Charge More for Happier Clients

Ken Edzerza is a First Nations businessman who has worked for over 30 years for different government departments helping at risk youth and serious young offenders overcome their challenges and become contributing members of society. When the parole office or family services doesn't know what to do with a troubled youth, or can't find one of their clients, they call Ken. Ken and I started working together because he needed to find a different business model. Despite obtaining a Masters in Leadership, Ken, like many business owners, lacked specialized knowledge around pricing his services and was underpaid and underappreciated for the important work he was doing as a result. Ken wanted to be paid fairly for his years of dedication, experience, and education. He thought he was worth three times what he was currently making from his business. While keeping that number in mind and taking a structured approach to Ken's impressive skillset, we mapped out a plan to raise his rates and move away from his hourly wage. Happily, Ken has more than hit his targets and, more importantly, he can afford to keep working in environments where he feels appreciated, can use his skills to empower at risk youth to enjoy better lives, and has opportunities to train others to do the same. As a result, Ken has made a difference in many more lives, made a transformation in his community, and made more money with his business.

Raise Your Prices

Many business owners balk at the thought of raising their prices and undervalue what they sell as a result. Yet, throughout all of history (and still in many marketplaces), negotiating or haggling price was commonplace. The "one price policy" was introduced with the development of large scale retailing at the end of the 19th century, but it definitely isn't the best model for small business owners (Kolter, 2007). The issue of how to best price your products and services is complicated by the use of the internet and software designed to give the consumer the lowest price possible at any given moment. **So how do we determine the best possible pricing that will benefit the business and not just the customer?** As we will discuss further, discounting is just a rush to the bottom of the barrel and will result in business failure. **In 30 years in business, I have seen more businesses fail as a result of pricing their products too low than from pricing them too high.** That being said, there is a fine balance between pricing your products too low and pricing them too high. Luckily, there are many pricing strategies that entrepreneurs can use to ensure their viability, while filling the needs of their customers.

Everyone Wants Value, Not a Deal

To understand how to best price our products, we need to consider how people buy. Research has shown that consumers make purchase decisions based on their perception of value. This value is determined by the information that customers receive through their senses, advertising, communication, and conversations with families, friends, and coworkers. Fortunately for us, **there is research that suggests that consumers cannot recall prices accurately**

(Dickenson, 1990). If this were not so, it truly would be a case of who could provide the lowest prices. **Happily, consumers buy based on more than just price. Most consumers take into consideration the perceived value of the product. We can influence perceived value as business owners by how we reference our selling price.** We can do this a number of ways such as how we situate our products in relation to our competition, showcasing our range of offerings. I always suggest that, if possible, business owners have 3 reference points or service offerings: a low, medium, and premium pricing model. Dan Ariely in his book, *Predictably Irrational,* found that giving three options increased revenue by a whopping 43 percent (Ariely, 2008). Too many options can confuse the customer and lead to fewer sales. If your customers are buying based on value, they may automatically choose your premium-priced product, while others will gravitate to your low-priced model. Your sales scripts and pricing model will help you determine the best product to sell to that customer.

Pricing Options

There are a variety of options in how we can price our products. For example, boutiques might pick a higher value-priced model. Some business models demand a discount strategy. For some businesses (including many in manufacturing), it might be a commodity-demand pricing model that they follow. In his book Priced to Sell: A Complete Guide to More Profitable Pricing, Herman Holtz says that **the best price is "the highest one that fits your business's strategy"** (Holtz, 1996). In other words, you should be pricing your products to fit the model of your business, which we described in chapter 4. Ideally, you want to differentiate your products and services from your competitors enough to justify different prices. Hopefully, the pricing model that you pick is going to be one that will allow you to be profitable.

The problem with most entrepreneurs and business managers is that they only consider one model of pricing. We don't often consider that we may be able to sell the same product or service to a different market or market segment at a different price. This new market might be geographical, socioeconomic, or use-based. When this happens, we can often adapt our pricing to reflect the market conditions in the new opportunity. Sometimes we can use opportunity pricing to increase our margins during times of higher demand. Of course, any time we consider changes in pricing, we need to think about the effect that this will have on our customers. **However, if we are short-sighted and fail to consider these different opportunities, our business will lose the potential for this revenue over the long run and rob us of profits.**

Pricing Models

There are a number of pricing models that can lead to success in your business. I am going to list some of them here with a short description of each. **As you read through the pricing models, consider how you could implement them in your business.** Think about how they work and how it might change the way you do things. I can tell you that I have experimented with many of these pricing models. Every business needs a number of pricing strategies to optimize profits and ensure that your customers receive value.

Anchor Pricing: Jewellers know that the best way to sell a $5000 diamond ring is to put it beside a $15,000 comparative model. In this manner, your customers of the $5000 variety believe that they are getting great value. This psychological approach can put profit in your pocket. I have heard of at least one retailer who would advertise an incredibly expensive item (say, for example, a $700 Frisbee) to sell 500 of the $30 "premium" variety. This particular retailer said he didn't actually care if he sold the expensive one because people would come from all over just to look at it and, in doing so, would pick up a cheaper one that had great margin. Over time, someone would come in and buy the expensive one because some buyers just need to own that one-of-a-kind item!

Auction Type Pricing: We are all familiar with this age-old pricing model from services such as eBay. In this pricing model, the buyer determines the maximum amount that they are willing to pay for a product or service. This model only works for some sellers, in some markets, and may not be applicable to your business. The key to this type of selling is to have your desired profit margin built into your minimum selling price.

Branding Pricing: Many successful business owners use this pricing model. Branding pricing essentially means that you have at least 2 (and preferably 3) similar products in each category. You then price them according to: good, better, and best. In other words, when you have a customer shopping solely based on price, you sell them the lower priced "good" product. If you can move them up with your sales skills to the "better" or "best" products, you should be able to increase your margin. Note: most consumers are going to buy your middle priced product because they want more value than the good product without paying full price for the best product. Make sure your middle, or good, product is the one with the highest margin.

In his book *Priceless, The Hidden Psychology of Value*, William Poundstone discusses an experiment where beer drinkers were offered 2 types of beer: a premium beer for $2.50 and a bargain beer for $1.80. Almost 80% chose the premium beer. In a second experiment, a third option was added: a cheaper beer for only $1.60, a mid beer for $1.80, and the high priced beer at $2.50. Now, 80% bought the $1.80 beer and 20% bought the $2.50 beer. The total sales dropped by 18%.

In a third experiment, the cheapest beer was eliminated so that the low price beer was $1.80, the mid priced beer was $2.50, and a super premium beer for $3.50 was added. Something interesting happened! 90% bought the $2.50 beer and 10% bought the $3.50 beer. Total sales went up by 10%.

	Cheap Price	Medium Price	Premium Price	Total Sales $
Experiment 1	$1.80=20% sales		$2.50 =80%	
	$36		$200	$236
Experiment 2	$1.60=0% sales	$1.80=80%	$2.50=20	
		$144	$50	$194 (-18%)
Experiment 3	$1.80=0%	$2.50=90%	$3.50=10%	
		$225.	$35	$260 (+10%)

The point is, you will sell more if you have 3 choices. You should have a premium price as an anchor, and the product you want to sell most as the middle choice.

Bundle Pricing: Encourage your customers to buy more by putting products suited to your target market together in a package. If you can get better pricing from your suppliers for duo-packs, kits, or combinations, do it and watch your profit dollars increase. Bundle pricing can seriously amp up your sales.

Commodity Pricing: Sometimes called "going rate pricing". If you have commodity products, you probably need to ensure that some of your key commodity products are priced similarly to others in the market place. In other words, if there is a market price for the product that you sell (a going rate), and you cannot differentiate your product or service in any way that creates value for your customer, you need to follow this model. To increase profitability, you will need to focus on differentiating your product or service offerings to boost sales or reduce your costs to increase margins.

Discount Pricing: This is a rush to the bottom and a quick way to go out of business. My Father always told me that in sports, there is always someone who is going to come along who is faster, stronger, or better than you. Well, in business, there is always someone who is willing to sell for less than you! In some markets, competitors end up selling to customers for much less than the product is worth, believing that they have won a customer for life. Chances are, that lifetime value of the customer (or cost in this case), is limited by how long the business remains the cheapest in the market. If you want to have a long, profitable business career, stay away from getting into discount pricing unless you are simply using very select products.

Eliminate The Dollar Sign: Perhaps you might consider how you price your products. Depending on your business, you might want to eliminate the dollar sign. A pricing experiment published in a study by Cornell University found that restaurants that had the price listed as $24 or 24 Dollars sold significantly less than those where the price was just 24 (Yang 2009).

Geographic Pricing: The fact is, certain markets are willing to pay more for products. This is because there are a variety of factors that influence how much somebody is willing to pay for your product. One of the biggest is location! You will get a different price selling your pickup truck in Washington, D.C. vs. Montana. The same house in a different geographic location is going to sell for a different price. Consider what your market is willing to pay and price accordingly.

High/Low Pricing: You are already probably familiar with this pricing model. A business will have a regular high price, but put products on sale to encourage customers to come in and buy more frequently and in larger amounts, or impulse buy. I like this model combined with the Stack 'em High, Watch 'em Fly merchandising model, which has been proven to work for many businesses. In this case, you try to secure lower pricing from your supplier for a higher volume purchase in order to put products on sale. When you are doing this, however, try to get a guaranteed sale from your supplier, so that you can send back product that doesn't sell after a given period of time.

Premium Pricing: If you walk into a boutique, you know that you are probably going to be paying a higher price than a similar product in a grocery store. However, you are also going to get better service and a higher quality product. Sometimes, the perception of quality is enough to demand premium pricing. Are there things you can do to ensure better profit margins by selling premium priced products? Do you have unique brands, or can you brand your service offerings to be able to ask for more money from willing customers?

Prices Ending with 9: There is research to suggest that prices ending in 9 will outsell prices ending in 5 by up to 24% in some cases. Research published in the Quantitative Marketing and Economics Journal found that prices ending with a 9 increased demand (Anderson, 2003). Another study compared pricing between 88 endings, 99 endings, and 00 endings, and found that 99 price endings outsold 00 endings by 8% and 00 endings sold better than 88 endings by 1% (Schindler, 1996).

Retainer pricing: This is a valuable option for contract or bid pricing. The idea behind this type of pricing is that you move from an hourly rate to a monthly or annual rate for your services. This can increase your effective hourly rate and allow more flexibility for your customers and your business.

Seasonal Pricing: Everyone knows that the price you can get for a bouquet of nice flowers is going to be different in November than it will be on Valentine's Day or Mother's Day. Do you have products that are seasonal or in more demand at certain times? Can you figure out a way of getting more margin through your buying and pricing models?

Step Pricing: I have used this model in my stores with great success. When using this pricing model, you only use 2 or 4 ending points. For example, all of our products cost xx.29, xx.49, xx.79, and xx.99. In some categories we only use endings of 49 or 99. In the first case, anything over 00 would get priced at 29, anything over 30 would get priced at 49, anything over 50 would move to 79, and anything over 80 would get priced at 99. So, for example, you want to get a 40% gross margin, and you are using a mark-up of 1.66. If you had a $5 item, and you mark it up by multiplying by 1.66, you get $8.30. Using step pricing, anything over 30 would automatically go to 49, so your staff would price this item at $8.49, giving you almost $.19

extra profit and a 1% increase in margin. Using this type of pricing on a regular basis can make a difference to your bottom line. As my friend Deane Parkes likes to says, a 1% margin on $1 million in sales puts $10,000 in your pocket!

Subscription Pricing: Would you rather spend $1000 per year or $83.33 per month? Of course most buyers will choose the lower monthly amount, even though it ends up exactly the same over 12 months. How can you price your product or service in such a way that you increase the number of people who think that they can afford you?

Value Pricing: Ikea is a perfect example of this. They offer a fairly high quality product at a value to the consumer. Sometimes you will see businesses run an EDLP (Everyday Low Price) pricing model on products. If you can negotiate better pricing on select products from your suppliers, this is a good way of creating sales and maintaining margin.

Do it now!

What is holding you back from getting more money from your business?

What is your current pricing model?

Should you have different levels of pricing?

Are there models of pricing that you would like to explore?

List the types of pricing models that you would like to experiment with in some aspect of your business.

How and when are you going to implement pricing changes?

Health Tip for Business Owners: Reduce Cortisol

Cortisol is a function of our fight or flight response. When our body is subject to stress, it releases cortisol to help us cope. The problem is, when we put our bodies in stressful situations for days, weeks, months, or even years, as business owners sometimes do, the high cortisol levels can have serious effects. High cortisol levels in the body have been linked to:

- Blood sugar issues and diabetes

- Weight gain and belly fat

- Heart conditions

- Infertility

- Immune system suppression

Long-term elevated cortisol has also been linked to insomnia, thyroid disorders, dementia, depression, chronic fatigue syndrome, as well as other conditions.

If you are riding the rollercoaster of your business and are experiencing chronic stress, you need to find ways to reduce your stress levels if you want to preserve your health. A great supplement that has helped many of our customers struggling with the stress of daily life is Truehope EMP. This product has been clinically studied and proven to help you balance your mood and reduce anxiety! Get it at your local health food store or online at Truehope com.

Chapter 12: Crap Is Everywhere!

Reducing your expenses and overhead to increase profitability.

Warning: This story is not for those with queasy stomachs. If this is you, please proceed to the synopsis.

Business travel can be hazardous. Margaret was scheduled for a C-section for our third child on October 5, 2004, but, on the morning of October 4th, I was up early to catch the 6 am flight to Vancouver. I was part of the negotiating team for a group of retailers that was working together to reduce their expenses and create a sustainable business model in a changing retail environment. We had some meetings with suppliers scheduled for that morning.

The flight itself was uneventful and, as we approached Vancouver, I thought it would be best to use the bathroom before my day of meetings started. I made my way up the aisle in an old Dash 8 airplane. Squeezing myself through the door and sitting down, I immediately realized, as my knees touched the door, that I was now folded up in the world's smallest bathroom. Bumping into walls as I turned around in this coffin-sized lavatory, I eventually found the hidden toilet paper. As there was no sink, I cleaned my hands with the lemon-scented wipes and went back to my seat, put my seatbelt on, and prepared to land. With my elbow on the armrest and my fingers resting on my chin, I contemplated the upcoming day's events.

WHOA! What was that smell? My nostrils inhaled an odour definitely unlike the smell of flowers that hits you when you get off the plane in Hawaii. This smell was significantly different. It smelled like crap!

The pile of crap looked just like a small mountain on my finger! My eyes now must have bulged in horror because I didn't recognize the colour of that mountain as something that had come from me. This was definitely not mine! I remembered that I had stuffed a lemon scented wipe in my shirt pocket. I quickly cleaned the offending finger, wiped it thoroughly, and rested back in my chair. As we started to land, I was once again hit by the odour! I looked over to the thankfully empty seat next to me and saw some crap on it; I looked on my shirt ... the crap was there too; I looked at my belt... the crap seemed everywhere! It now became apparent that someone else had had trouble finding the toilet paper in that indoor outhouse!

I almost bolted off the plane as it landed, hoping that no one else had noticed what was going on. I headed for the second set of bathrooms (the first bathrooms are always full when you come off a plane at this time of the morning) and cleaned up with lots of soap and water. Figuring that I had done a pretty good job of my laundry, I headed to the pickup zone where my friend Boyd was waiting. Boyd's smiling face turned to a questioning one as he saw my water-logged state and asked about my wet clothes. "It's a long story," I said, not wanting to talk about it. "I will tell you another time."

Synopsis: We need to look everywhere in our business when we are hoping to clean up the crappy expenses that are making our profit and loss statement smell bad. This chapter will help you clean up your profit and loss or income statement and put that money into your pocket!

A Business in Trouble

When Mother Maria's Market opened in 1999, it had a number of partners and was multifaceted. The market was a mixture of organic and conventional grocery products, and fresh and frozen dairy and meats. There was a large vitamin, skin care, and a gift section. With 7000 square feet of selling area, the store also had a deli, bakery, coffee shop, and cappuccino bar that was staffed by several people at all times. The store was open from early morning to late at night to serve the hordes of customers that we hoped would be clambering for our products.

Problems started before the store was even finished. There were cost overruns, wiring issues, and refrigeration equipment problems that were exacerbated by a poor choice of contractors. A new, partially customized Point of Sale system couldn't function quickly enough to ensure reliability. On top of this, some department managers had personality conflicts, and we had a poor physical business location.

It is not uncommon for businesses to experience some of these issues when starting up. Hopefully, the owners can get them under control quickly enough to avoid bankruptcy.

Our marketing drew in customers once the store was opened. In fact, on some days, we had so many customers coming through the doors that we couldn't keep up! But the business kept losing money; we lost $278,000 in the first 12 months! What went wrong? It was all on the financial statements:

1. Average sales were too low at just $9 (about ⅓ of our other store).

2. Labour costs were too high; we had higher labour costs for fewer sales than our other operation.

3. Gross margins were way too low. In the bakery, we had to replace our original idea of scratch baking with a ready-bake model that had lower labour costs but also lower margins. We were unable to produce enough unique products with high enough margins to make the business profitable. Other areas of the business also had lower margins than we were used to and needed, all affecting our profitability.

4. A high waste level due to regular equipment failures and waste from the deli, bakery, and produce departments killed our business profits.

5. Old equipment skyrocketed energy and utility costs.

6. Uncompetitive suppliers meant some of our supply costs were 50%, which was higher than they should have been.

7. Poor staffing decisions and too many managers resulted in personality conflicts and an overabundance of labour.

8. To provide a benefit for our employees, we covered some food costs, but these were eventually reduced, and then eliminated to save money.

9. We exceeded our line of credit on a regular basis, resulting in high bank charges.

It took the second year to turn the business around. We eliminated positions and scaled back on parts of the operation that were unfeasible. We cut costs by eradicating several parts of the store that relied on fresh product, and replaced them with another business model. We reduced our energy costs and sold off our old equipment. We started selling antiques that we purchased or received on consignment. These changes enabled us to make more money with less labour and finally turn a profit. When our lease was up, we reduced our size by 80% and kept the profitable parts of the business. The business is profitable to this day!

Lean!

Lean is a concept that was made popular in Japan, but is transferable to small businesses worldwide. The idea is that a business can lower expenses and become profitable as a result of "just-in-time" inventory, high-quality products, and business synchronisation to reduce waste. For a small business, this means doing things right the first time. Carry minimal inventory that will maximize sales, and motivate your staff to look for ways to reduce expenses throughout the business operations. Waste can usually be found in four areas:

1. **Transitions**: Regular ordering along with smooth transitions and processes between departments can reduce and even eliminate waste.

2. **Supply:** Make sure that you are ordering just enough and just in time without compromising sales or holding extra inventory. Losing sales because you don't have adequate supply or losing money because you have it tied up in inventory are examples of waste common to many businesses.

3. **Business Systems:** Doing things the way they have always been done and selling things the way they have always been sold could be costing you money. You should always be flexible in your business. If your customer has requirements that are different from your regular specs, consider how you can deliver to their requirements and still make a profit.

4. **Quality:** Your product or service needs to be perfect each and every time. When you have to redo things, you waste time, energy, and money. Putting systems in place to ensure that your employees perform their duties as near to perfection as possible each and every time will ensure that you reduce waste and increase profits.

Where to Reduce Expenses

When we are cleaning up our income and expense sheet in search of increased profitability, we need to look for the crap that is everywhere. If we have put our own money into the business from start-up, we are usually more inclined to make sure that expenses are low. I have noticed that if there are outside investors, business managers without incentives to keep costs down can often burn through cash. Even when business owners are part of the day-to-day operation, they can pad expenses in areas where they don't want to be bothered, instead of looking for less expensive alternatives. When things are good we forget to wipe expenses off. We have extra supplies, extra inventory, extra services, extra advertising, extra stuff that is doing nothing for our businesses. I have seen some owners fly first class and take vacations on company expenses. They eat lavishly when times are good, and use company cars and assets for their families without thought. Faced with recession, a downturn in the business, or a profitability problem, the attention gets brought back to reducing expenses. Sometimes, however, we forget to look in areas where we might be able to increase profitability with a few adjustments to how we spend the money our business sales have generated. Here are some ideas on how you can reduce your expenses!

107 Ways You Can Reduce Your Expenses

Cash Management:

1. Look for cash discounts from your supplier.
2. Hold cash as long as possible if there are no discounts.
3. Require two signatures on all cheques, contracts, etc.
4. Charge interest on overdue payments from customers.
5. Credit cards must be paid on time to avoid charges.
6. Avoid issuing company credit cards to employees.
7. Consider contracting out payroll services.
8. Avoid late payments to suppliers to avoid penalties.

9. Set up alerts for scheduling payments.
10. Read your statements regularly to monitor cash flow.
11. Avoid giving credit to your customers whenever possible – you are not their bank.
12. Have a vibrant A/R collection process to improve cash flow.
13. Check the rates you are being charged for accepting credit cards, and ask regularly for better pricing.

Accounting and Insurance:

14. Get multiple insurance quotes on a regular basis.
15. Consider self-insurance programs for employee health benefits.
16. Raise deductibles to lower insurance costs.
17. Ask your insurance agent what you can do in your business to reduce risk and get better rates.
18. Consider in-house bookkeeping.
19. Ask your accountant for a reduced rate.
20. Make sure to take the time with your accountant to get a clear financial understanding of your business.

Advertising:

21. Review your advertising costs quarterly and measure against results.
22. Contact vendors for co-op dollars for advertising spending.
23. Never advertise just because everybody else does it - have a plan.
24. Cut your advertising budget in half for 1 year and see what happens.
25. Try new, cheaper advertising methods.
26. Start a blog.
27. Use Facebook, LinkedIn, and other social media - if you can maintain them.
28. Use YouTube for promotion.
29. Start an e-newsletter.

30. Bag-stuff your customers with information and offers that will bring them back into your business.
31. Give free seminars to your customers using your staff and vendors as speakers.
32. Try to get free publicity!

Consulting Fees:

33. Review all consulting fees regularly.
34. Consider contracting out those things that are costing you money and labour.
35. Pay consultants for training your staff in sales for better results.
36. Consider free training from people just starting out in the consulting business and looking for gigs.
37. Watch for creeping costs in consulting, and entertain hiring your consultant as an employee if this will save you money.
38. Hire freelancers who will work at home and reduce your costs.

Inventory:

39. Monitor your turns and use inventory systems to have just-in-time inventory practices.
40. Sell off unused inventory at reduced prices to turn that inventory into cash.
41. Put products on sale before expiry dates.
42. Smart buying can save you money, but don't overbuy because something is on sale. Always use your inventory system to gauge how much you can sell over the next period.
43. Train your staff who are ordering your inventory to adhere to your system and to make smart choices.

Lease and Rent:

44. Look for ways to reduce your rent and lease costs. Ask for reduced rates.
45. Consider your long-term strategic plan before entering extended leases.

46. Look for ways to purchase your building or site as a way to reduce costs and increase your investments.
47. Reduce the size of your rental space by eliminating products that don't sell and focusing on your key products.
48. Operate your business out of your house, if you can.

Meals and Entertainment:

49. Consider giving your staff per diem rates instead of blanket coverage of meals.
50. Eliminate the alcohol - many companies no longer pay for their staff to drink, and neither should you.
51. Find ways to get your suppliers to take your staff out for training dinners.
52. Consider potluck dinners for company events.

Memberships:

53. Review your memberships regularly to see if you are benefiting from them.
54. Make the most of association benefits to reduce insurance, travel, and shipping costs.
55. At trade shows and association events, have a plan to come away with a money-making idea.
56. Look for opportunities to join buying groups or alliances to reduce costs.

Repairs and Maintenance:

57. Keep track of your equipment by asking contractors to sign a sheet that is attached to the equipment each time it is serviced.
58. Eliminate equipment that is costing you in repairs and replace it with new or slightly used alternatives.
59. Get multiple quotes on expensive repairs.
60. Learn to fix stuff yourself.
61. Find contractors that will work at lower rates for smaller projects.

Supplies:

62. Only buy products in bulk if you will be using them on a very regular basis. Don't buy 2 year's worth of anything.
63. Go paperless if you can.
64. Get a service contract for photocopiers and printers to reduce expensive toner pricing.
65. Keep track of supplies to avoid employee home use.
66. Check your pricing of office suppliers.

Travel Expenses:

67. Avoid travel whenever possible to reduce costs.
68. Use technology for meetings where possible.
69. Never fly first class. Instead, use budget hotels and airlines where possible, and save the fancy flying for when you travel with your family.
70. Book early or use points.
71. Have one staff member travel instead of a whole group and get them to come back and present what they learned.

Utilities:

72. Avoid company cell phone issued to employees. Pay lump sums on a monthly basis to avoid contracts and reduce abuse.
73. Consider VOIP phone services to reduce costs.
74. Consider eliminating your landlines.
75. Eliminate extra phone services that you no longer use or need.
76. Save energy by painting with bright colors and utilizing natural light.
77. Turn your computers off at night, and you will save $50 per computer, per year.
78. Turn off air conditioners and heaters when there is no one in your building to save energy.
79. Change your filters regularly to reduce energy usage.
80. Buy only energy efficient equipment when replacing or investing.

81. Get a free energy audit.
82. Look for energy credits for reducing your load.
83. Replace expensive energy-burning lights with new efficient ones.
84. Use technology to reduce energy costs.
85. Search for inexpensive local web hosting.
86. Use cloud storage instead of local servers to reduce energy cost.

Vehicles:

87. Buy used vehicles for your company whenever possible to reduce loss of investment.
88. Have logbooks for vehicles to ensure proper use.
89. Eliminate collision insurance on older vehicles to reduce costs.
90. Trade vehicle repairs for your goods and services.
91. Consider offering mileage rates to your staff instead of buying company vehicles.

Wages and Benefits:

92. Review your scheduling hours on a weekly basis.
93. Consider cutting your hours of operation by looking closely at your customer activities and times of patronage.
94. Offer wellness days and unpaid leave to staff members who you want to keep on and are a blessing to your business.
95. Review your staff compensation on a regular basis to ensure that it is fair and to avoid staff turnover.
96. Consider profit sharing programs to incentivize staff.
97. Be slow to hire and quick to fire.
98. Have regular employee performance reviews to ensure that they are focused on their job and know what is expected of them.
99. Consider interns or crowdsourcing where possible to reduce your costs.
100. Stagger working hours to ensure your business is adequately staffed during the times that your customers need your help.

101. Close on holidays or days when business is slow.
102. Send staff home when it's slow by asking who would like to take the rest of the day off.
103. Outsource HR and payroll to external providers when feasible to save money.
104. Consider part-time employees when possible. This can result in labour cost savings in some cases, and give you additional capacity when needed.

Waste:

105. Price your waste contracts on an annual basis.
106. Recycle as much as possible.
107. Look at where your company creates waste, and try to eliminate it at the source.

The key to reducing expenses is to regularly review changes on your income statement. Why have certain things changed? What are you doing differently? By operating in a lean fashion, you can reduce your debt levels or save money right to your pocket.

Health Tip for Business Owners: Expert Doctors

Health insurance for business owners sometimes covers visits to massage therapists, reflexologists, acupuncturists, and naturopathic physicians. Consider finding new ways to deal with chronic issues that are bothering you! You might just be surprised at what really works!

Chapter 13: Your Monthly Report Card

How to determine if you are actually making money!

My brothers and I would sometimes get into trouble both at school and at home. Though we generally had good grades, my mother would always make a point of reading our report cards as soon as we brought them home. Walking home from school on that warm day in June, when I was in Grade 7 and Rob in Grade 6 was a particularly satisfying walk. Not only would I be headed to high-school the next year, but (to our delight) we found a garter snake trying to get across the road on the way home. Garter snakes are fairly common and not harmful but, if you don't like snakes, they can be terrifying. Rob quickly scooped up the snake that was about 18 inches long and, having no bag to stick it in, dumped it into the yellow manila envelope holding his report card. Reaching the house, we burst into the kitchen and proudly presented our poor unsuspecting mother our report cards. It was all fine and good until Mom reached her hand into Rob's envelope. The unfortunate snake seized its chance for freedom and slithered up mom's arm almost giving her a heart attack. Rob and I almost split our guts laughing as we tried to avoid

Mom's swipes at us with a wooden spoon. Grabbing the snake, we headed out the back door to avoid any further repercussions and released the snake back into nature.

Synopsis: Report cards are as important in business as they are in school. Knowing how to read your report card is essential for keeping your business profitable. Sometimes, as kids, we were scared to read our report cards. This chapter is going to help you understand your reports and hopefully guide you on your way to reports that are always full of good news.

No Reports and No Cash

Cassandra contacted me after I had given a presentation to a group of business owners. She and her husband were the proprietors of a hardware business, but their interests lay elsewhere. They had turned over the business to be run by her brother-in-law. After two years, the brother-in-law decided that he didn't want to manage the business anymore and quit. This left Cassandra in a pickle. She and her husband and their kids had already left town and relocated 700 miles away. Upon returning to the business, she realized that the accounts were in a mess. Taxes had not been filed, year-ends had not been completed, and the bank account was running on empty. The business's sales were falling and, as a result, Cassandra and her husband could no longer maintain their lifestyle. They had never needed to look at financial statements before. They had thought that everything was fine, but had inadvertently been draining the bank account. Now the flow had stopped. What should they do?

You Need a Report Card!

If you are in business, you need a report card. Many business owners I know look at the only statement that means anything to them: their bank statement. Often, they don't even look at this statement

What You Need To Know About Your Statement

Sales Income – Revenue: Are sales increasing or decreasing? By what percentage? Do you have certain departments that are growing or declining compared to the previous period? Why is that happening? What are the trends in the business? Are you doing anything differently that is helping or hurting sales? Why are certain areas outperforming others? The more you can figure this out, the better chance you have of being successful.

Cost of Goods Sold: Look at each line on your income statement. What has changed from the previous period? Can you explain the changes? Is there any input cost that you can reduce?

Gross Profit: Look at the gross profit percentage compared to the previous period. Has it gone up or down? If the gross profit has gone down, you may need to make changes to ensure this does not continue. What needs to be done? If it is going up, good for you. Consider what you have done to make this happen. Can you continue to do this?

General and Administrative Expenses: Carefully compare this area line by line to the previous period. Are there expenses that have gone up? Why have they gone up? What needs to be changed? Are there areas where you can eliminate more costs? Remember that every unnecessary cost that you can reduce goes directly into your pocket as an owner!

Profit: Compare your profit in this period to the previous period. Are you going in the right direction? Have you hit your goal for your profit? Are you happy with this number or discouraged? What needs to happen for you to reach your goals? Remember, you own the business to make a profit. This area is especially important!

as they just check their bank balance when they are doing a deposit. Many small business owners base their important decisions on what is in the bank on any given day. This is problematic. You are asking for trouble if you do not know where you are coming from, where you are going, or how well your business is doing. This is like driving a car without a gas gauge or a sports team not finding out until the end of the season if they have won or lost games during the season. **You wouldn't play sports or games without keeping score. Why play roulette with your business by not keeping score? Make it a point now of keeping track.** As my friend Ed Graydon, a multimillionaire who built his fortune in the monitoring business, likes to say, "What gets measured is meaningful."

Who Does Your Books?

When it comes to financial statements, many business owners leave it up to their accountants to tell them how they are doing. Often, these statements are viewed only at tax time or year end. Accountants, on the other hand, are looking at the statements with different eyes than most business owners should be. An accountant's job is to ensure that the company is compliant with the tax laws. Rarely does an accountant go through the statement line by line and give you a synopsis of what is working and not working for you. The problem with this picture in the first place, is that often these statements are 3-6 months out of date. The second problem is that most business owners only want to know how much taxes they must pay and by when.

I am shocked at the number of business owners who tell me that their bookkeeping is months or even years behind! How can you ever tell if you are making money if your bookkeeping is not up-to-date? How do you know what areas of your business are improving or declining? How do you know that your staff is not stealing from you? Your financial statements are your report card that show you how your business is doing. If you are serious about making your business profitable, you need to do three things each and every month.

1. You need to start asking your bookkeeper for printed **Monthly Comparative Financial Statements!** If you don't have a bookkeeper – get one. If you are doing the bookkeeping yourself and you love it - do it. But print off hard copies that you can write on. You should be reading these statements before the end of the following month. In other words, you need to be reading your January financials in February.

2. The second thing you need to do is **read your statements and note the differences** in your operation from year to year.

3. Know your breakeven point. Knowing what you need to break even is important for business owners. This breakeven point should include your profit goal.

What Is The Income Statement And Why Is It Important?

For some small business owners, income statements are going to be the first statement they need to look at. Your income statement is a recording of a given period (usually a month or a year) of your business sales minus your expenses, showing you your profit or loss for the period. A statement is broken down as follow:

Income Statement

Sales	January ($)	February ($)	% Change
Cost of Sales	52,538	54,639	+3.9
Food Cost	12546	13132	+4.6
Liquor Cost	3215	4352	+35.36
Total Cost of Goods Sold	15761	17484	+11
Gross Profit	36777	37154	+1

Gross Profit %	70%	68%	-2
Operating Expenses			
Owner's Salary	5000	5000	0
Wages & Benefits	17605	18985	+7.8
Advertising	713	921	+29
Legal & Accounting	200	50	-75
Supplies	805	713	-11.5
Entertainment	3000	3250	+8.3
Utilities	2441	2527	+3.5
Insurance	207	207	0
Interest	644	641	-1
Depreciation	541	541	0
Repairs	1100	695	-37
Total Operating Expenses	32256	33530	+3.9
Operating Profits	4521	3624	-20
Break-even Point Total Operating Expenses Divided by GM%	46,080	49,308	

Now imagine if you were focused on these numbers on a regular basis. Once you understand how to read the income statement, it should only take you a few minutes to determine part of the health of your business. The other part of the report card is the balance sheet and the cash flow sheet.

Comparative Balance Sheet

January 31st

Assets	2016	2015
Cash	41 000	47 000
Accounts Receivable	30,000	34,000
Prepaid Expenses	4,000	3,000
Total Current Assets	75,000	84,000
Land	50,000	31,000
Building	102,000	83,000
Equipment	52,000	41,000
Accumulated Depreciation	(24,000)	(12,000)
Total Assets	253,000	227000

Liabilities:

Accounts Payable	20,000	16,000
Long Term Notes Payable	29,000	19,000
Common Stock	100,000	100,000
Retained Earnings	104,000	92,000
Total Liabilities	253,000	227,000

Your balance sheet is a snapshot of your company at a specific point in time. Let's say this date is December 31, 20xx. By looking at the balance sheet, you can tell how much you own. These are called your ASSETS. You will also be able to tell how much you owe. These are your LIABILITIES. Finally there is a section called EQUITY. This simply means how much investment you or others have in the company.

The reason this statement is called a balance sheet is because it is supposed to balance. In other words, **ASSETS = LIABILITY + EQUITY**

What Can You Learn From Reading Your Balance Sheet?

Balance sheets are important tools for owners. For example, reviewing the assets on your balance sheet can prompt the following questions:

1. How much cash do you have in the bank? How does this compare to the previous statement date? If your cash is dwindling, why? If your cash is increasing, by how much?

2. Is accounts receivable increasing or decreasing? If it's increasing, why are your customers using you as a bank more often? It is important to ask your bookkeeper for an accounts receivable statement. This will be broken down into columns of 30, 60, 90, and 180 days. Look at the amounts in each column and come up with a strategy to get customers to pay you faster. This might be providing calling scripts for your staff, so they know exactly what to say and when.

3. Is your inventory increasing or decreasing? Why? Do you need this much inventory or do you need more to ensure your customers are able to buy your product when they need it? Again, how does it compare to the previous statement? Do you have systems in place that will ensure that you always have optimal inventory in stock?

Cash Flow Statements

Sometimes I work with owners who have profitable businesses but are short on cash. This can be a result of a number of factors, but is most often related to uncollected accounts receivables. However, there are other factors that affect cash.

A cash flow statement looks at cash that is generated through three activities:

1. **Operations:** This is how much cash is coming in (sales) and going out (expenses) from your business.

Balance Sheets

Assets: Your assets are everything your business owns. Sometimes this is broken down into two sections: current assets and fixed assets.

Current Assets: Current assets can be converted into cash quickly. Common examples are cash, accounts receivable (money you are owed by your customers), investments, prepaid expenses and inventory.

Fixed Assets: Fixed assets, like office furniture, equipment, vehicles, land, and buildings take longer to be turned into cash. (Remember, it doesn't matter if you still owe money on these things - that will be considered in the liability section.)

Liabilities: Liabilities are everything you owe. These are broken down further into: current liabilities and long-term debt.

Current Liabilities: Accounts payable (what you owe to suppliers), income taxes, and lease payments are all current liabilities. They are things you need to pay in the short term.

Long-Term Debt: Business loans are long-term debt. Perhaps you bought land or equipment and are paying these off. This is where you look to see how much you still owe.

Equity: The value of the ownership of the company is equity. This is broken into two sections as well: owner's equity and retained earnings.

Owner's Equity: Owner's equity typically lists shareholders by name and the amount that they have invested in the company and will need to be repaid. This may be by share type.

Retained Earnings: Retained earnings is money that the business has made over time that has been reinvested in the business in some way.

2. **Investing:** This part of the statement looks at where your cash is going in terms of investments. If you buy new equipment or put money into a term deposit, you lose cash. If you sell a vehicle or building or cash in a term deposit, you will increase your cash flow.

3. **Financing:** This area of the statement looks at where your cash is coming from and going in terms of financing. Did you get a bank loan or are you paying off a shareholder's loan? Did you, as an owner, take a draw, or did you pay dividends? Did you have to put more money into your company?

By looking at and understanding your cash flow statements on a regular basis you will get a clearer idea of where cash is coming from and where it is going. If your business is cash strapped, you should be doing this on a monthly basis. Read the statement so that you are completely clear about how your business is functioning.

Cash Flow Statement

Cash Flow Statement	May 31st ($)
Cash from Operations	
Earnings	9,110.00
Additions to Cash	
Depreciation	3200.00
Increase in Accounts Payable	4505.00
Increase in Taxes Payable	750.00
Decrease in Cash	
Accounts Receivable Increase	5500.00
Increase in Inventory	6500.00
Net Cash Provided by Operations	5,565.00
Cash From Investing	
Equipment	3225.00

Cash Flow from Financing	
Loan Repayment	2000.00
Change in Cash for Period	$ 340.00

As we can see from this simple cash flow statement, there are a number of things that affect our cash flow in the business. These can be positive like increasing profits, decreasing our inventory, reducing our accounts receivables, or increasing our accounts payables. If our cash is going down we can look in the opposite direction. Did we spend money on equipment or repay loans? Did our accounts receivables increase or our accounts payable decrease? Did we pay more taxes?

Other Things You Need to Measure

In the following list, the highlighted lines are those that the owner must look at regularly, and the remaining items need to be measured and reviewed by your management team.

Daily

1. Customer counts
2. Average sale
3. Conversion rates – how many people are you not able to sell to?
4. Project tracking
5. Sales leads and conversions

Weekly

6. Hotlist of prospective customers
7. Delivery timelines of product to customers
8. Out-of-stock levels
9. **Accounts receivable aging**
10. **Accounts payable**
11. **Cash requirements for the upcoming week**

12. **Credit card balances**
13. **Inventory levels**
14. **Bank deposit listings balanced to end-of-day reports**

Monthly

15. **Income statement**
16. **Balance sheet**
17. **Accounts receivable aging**
18. **Accounts payable update**
19. Project updates and scheduling
20. Cash flow statement
21. **Gross margin**
22. **Monthly average sales**
23. **Sales per square foot**
24. Hotlist of prospective customers
25. Top customers and their purchases
26. Returns and customer dissatisfaction levels
27. Waste and write offs
28. **Inventory levels**
29. Marketing results in comparison to cost

Any other key performance indicators that are specific to the delivery of product or services to your customers are always essential. **Remember that what is measured gets managed!**

How much profit should I be making?

A great way to find out how much profit is typical for your industry is to ask your association for benchmarking numbers. Additionally, some industry standards are listed below. Find one that is similar to yours and compare.

	Accom-modation	Accounting services	Advertising Services	Agricultural	Amusement
Sales	100%	100	100	100	100

Cost of Sale	11.13	12.37	30.03	43.77	22.04
Gross Profit	88.87	87.63	69.97	56.23	77.96
Rent	4.46	4.64	3.61	5.8	5.46
Advertising	2.85	2.69	2.59	0.45	2.03
Total Labour	25.07	41.28	23.74	8.68	21.76
Total Expense	75.95	78.36	62.24	46.29	66.05
Net Profit	12.52	9.7	7.73	9.94	11.94

	Banking	Beverage Manufacture	Broadcasting	Building Construction	Car Dealers
Sales	100%	100	100	100	100
Cost of sales	8.7	42.91	19.21	77.18	85.6
Gross Profit	91.3	57.09	80.79	22.82	14.4
Rent	3.96	0.79	1.8	0.74	0.94
Advertising	0.37	3.95	2.99	0.31	1
Total Labour	40.67	8.57	11.96	5.12	5.72
Total Expense	84.35	39.4	72.6	15.33	12.76
Net Profit	6.95	17.6	8.19	7.49	1.64

	Clothing Manufacture	Clothing stores	Computer Design	Education	Electronic Stores
Sales	100%	100	100	100	100
Cost of sale	61.5	51.54	28.09	13.44	69.24
Gross Profit	38.42	48.46	71.91	86.56	30.76
Rent	2.18	7.04	2.35	6.15	2.32
Advertising	2.22	2.4	0.032	6.13	2.22
Total Labour	10.91	15.91	29.78	32.7	11.69
Total Expense	31.3	40.48	63.22	74.95	26.08
Net Profit	7.12	7.98	8.69	11.61	4.68

	Engineering Construction	Engineering Services	Entertainment	Equipment manufacture	Food Manufacture
Sales	100%	100	100	100	100
Cost of sale	70.01	40	14.59	68.02	62.6
Gross Profit	29.99	59.92	85.41	31.98	37.46
Rent	2.16	3.05	2.84	2.77	1.34
Advertising	0.19	0.34	2.04	1.03	2.87
Total Labour	6.36	26.07	26.9	4.72	5.36

Total Expense	21.15	53.43	70.83	25.17	25.97
Net Profit	8.84	6.49	14.58	6.81	11.43

	Food Services	Foodstore	Forestry Logging	Gas Station	General Store
Sales	100%	100	100	100	100
Cost of sale	37.7	71.6	61.89	88.22	69.33
Gross Profit	62.3	28.32	38.11	11.74	30.67
Rent	6.52	2.02	1.42	0.96	2.19
Advertising	2.35	0.63	16	0.11	1.45
Total Labour	20.98	10.42	7.52	3.52	10.98
Total Expense	54.22	25.32	30.14	10.1	25.76
Net Profit	8	3	7.97	1.68	4.91

	Hardware store	Healthcare	Home store	Insurance	ISP
Sales	100%	100	100	100	100
Cost of sale	63.66	8.7	57.11	29.99	10.12
Gross Profit	36.34	91.3	42.89	70.71	89.88
Rent	2.96	3.86	4.78	2.26	3.22
Advertising	1.52	0.37	4.54	0.55	4.33
Total Labour	15.23	40.67	14.69	10	19.48
Total Expense	31.89	84.35	38.31	52.84	81.01
Net Profit	4.45	0.95	4.58	17.87	8.87

	Legal Services	Oil Gas Extraction	Outdoor Recreation	Power Generation	Publishing
Sales	100%	100	100	100	100
Cost of sale	6.78	44.24	56.72	56.75	22.96
Gross Profit	93.22	55.76	43.28	43.25	77.04
Rent	5.15	0.085	2.46	1.94	1.62
Advertising	2.09	0.03	0.46	0.09	3.02
Total Labour	47	4.11	9.84	4.08	22.63
Total Expense	81.84	30.69	35.33	8.07	59.83
Net Profit	12.18	25.07	7.95	5.18	17.21

	Renting leasing	Research develop	Staffing services	Telecom-munications	Trades Contractor
Sales	100%	100	100	100	100

Cost of sale	19.68	36.3	5.02	13.49	65.86
Gross Profit	80.32	63.7	44.98	86.51	34.14
Rent	5.85	2.85	0.93	5.06	2.06
Advertising	0.79	0.59	0.35	1.7	0.37
Total Labour	14.14	19.72	24.4	12.5	11.33
Total Expense	69.42	52.05	41.94	75.52	28.2
Net Profit	10.9	11.65	3.04	10.99	5.94

	Transportation	Travel Services	TV Audio	Utilities	Waste Mgt
Sales	100%	100	100	100	100
Cost of sale	31.94	35.57	24.75	28.81	39.17
Gross Profit	68.06	64.43	75.25	71.19	60.83
Rent	5.98	1.77	5.03	1.35	2.66
Advertising	0.24	4.33	2.92	0.25	0.34
Total Labour	19	5.93	12.18	7.37	15.62
Total Expense	63.53	51.53	64.48	62.29	53.13
Net Profit	4.53	12.9	10.77	8.9	7.7

	Wholesale Trade	Wood Manufacture			
Sales	100%	100			
Cost of sale	77.3	70.92			
Gross Profit	22.7	29.08			
Rent	1.09	0.97			
Advertising	1.07	0.55			
Total Labour	7.37	7.62			
Total Expense	18.45	22.13			
Net Profit	4.26	6.95			

Source: (Financial-Projections.com, 2016)

Do It Now!

Make a list of the financial reports you should review on a regular basis to ensure that you increase your profitability.

Who can deliver these reports to you, and what needs to be done to ensure that you get them in a timely manner?

Do you need more information to fully understand your reporting? Where can you get help?

What is your profit percentage?

What is your break-even point?

How much money do you owe?

List a few ways you would like to save money:

Organization Reports Chart

Here is an organizational Chart for a typical small business with reports that need to be considered for each position.

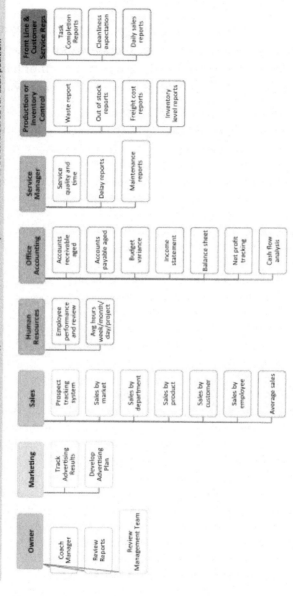

Health Tip for Business Owners: Henry Ford Used Meditation and Maybe You Should Too!

Meditate for better profits! Did you know that Henry Ford would start his day with 10 minutes of silent meditation to prepare him for a stressful day? If he could take ten minutes out of his busy morning and notice significantly better results, why can't you? Science now proves that taking a few minutes a day to concentrate on your breathing can allow you to be more productive and more peaceful!

Chapter 14: Too Old To Play In the Sandbox

When to get out of business, and how to ensure

you have a valuable business to sell!

"If you are over 40, the chances of you breaking a bone while snowboarding are significant," said my friend and surgeon Dr. Jamie Appleby as we rode the ski lift up into the sunshine. I was determined to defy those odds despite being well into my forties at that point. In fact, I thought myself to be somewhat of a 'natural' since I picked up the sport quickly when taught by my teenage daughters. Yet, the very next run proved me wrong. Boarding behind Jamie, who was making beautiful tracks through the snow on his skis, I caught an edge at high speed, spun around, and smashed my head on the ground (saved from permanent brain damage by my helmet). The concussion lasted for weeks. After a second fall on the snowboard a couple months later, I gave up the sport for good. I realized that I truly was too old to play in that sandbox.

Synopsis: I am not alone! Across North America and beyond, Baby Boomers are deciding, in droves, that they are either getting too old or they are too tired of playing in their current sandbox. However, very few of them have done the planning that's necessary to move out of the sandbox and into another playground.

So, What To Do with Your Business?

Mark called me from Toronto because he wanted some help transitioning his business. His exit strategy for his wildly successful electrical contracting business was to give the business to his son in the next 10 years. Mark had bought the business from his father and built up the business by focusing on commercial work with a select range of customers and a low cost business structure, and had reaped the rewards. While Mark was only in his early 50's and his son was 16, he had the foresight and wisdom to start thinking and planning for his retirement earlier rather than later. We started talking. Over the course of our sessions, it became clear that while Mark was ready to plan for his succession, some questions remained about his son. Not yet in the trades program and not having worked in the business, I asked Mark why he thought his son would like to take over. *"This business will set him up for life,"* said Mark. *"There are some questions about how my employees will take it, but I know that Jason is smart and will be able to handle it."* As we discussed it even further, I asked Mark what it was like to take over the business from his own father. He talked about the transition and how he had changed careers to take over the business. He noted that, while he had made lots of money, the daily grind of hard physical work, headaches, and employee issues was taking its toll. So I asked Mark, *"Is this what you want for your son?"* Mark was quiet for a long time. When he started to talk, his tone was different. *"You know, Dave, I need to think about this some more and really talk to my son. I am not even sure about what he really wants to do. I just assumed he would want this, and now I realize that I wouldn't want to wish this lifestyle on him."*

According to Lisë Stewart, founder of the Galliard Family Business Advisor Institute, there are many business owners giving up the sport of business; either they've been pushed out by family members or, as owners, have decided that they don't want to play anymore. The landscape of the business playground is changing. **In fact, Stewart says, conservatively, 55% of small and family-owned businesses are going to transition in the next 10 years, and those businesses are not prepared.** This poses big problems for owners and their families. Families are often broken up by the disagreements caused by the transfer of ownership in the business. Some families are already prone to this conflict because of family dynamics, but other families, who have a harmonious relationship, start to tear apart as the stress of ownership and need for profitability sets in. Siblings who might have gotten on well before, end up not talking to each other. In some cases, family members end up suing each other! Companies that were successful under the original ownership, break down and lose value with the new family members at the helm. If owners took the time to consider the issues surrounding the transition as they did in growing their businesses, there would be much less strife.

What Are The Two Big Issues?

1. **Who should take over the firm?** If you have more than one child, which one are you going to give or sell your business to? Parents need to think about this carefully. Lack of planning or foresight can result in considerable harm to the family dynamics. Do you want your kids to hate each other because they disagree about how to manage the money and assets of your business?

2. **Does your child or children have the aptitude** and interest for running your business? Stewart has plenty of examples of companies that dissolved, or were devalued, within a few years of ownership transfer because the children did not have the interest, skills, knowledge, or attitude to run the company as their parents did. You have built a great business, but a

wrong decision at your retirement could see all your hard work crumble.

What Do Owners Need To Do To Ensure A Successful Transition To The Next Generation?

Lisë Stewart says that within 2-3 years of a significant ownership transfer to the next generation, many companies begin to fail. This is because the children don't want the business or are not qualified. So, why do owners do it? Parents often believe that they are doing their very best for their children by bestowing on them titles, money, and power, not realizing that they can be setting their kids up for a lifetime of misery (Stewart, 2016). If the company fails and your children have only worked in the family business, where do they go? What will they do when the profits dry up and they have a fancy lifestyle to keep up without the generous help of the family business? This isn't to say that business can flourish when an experienced child takes over. However, if your heart is still set on transitioning your business to your children, here are some things that you should do:

A. **Start Talking About It**: What will the business look like for your children? Just like Mark the electrician, many owners have never had a good hard talk about their business exit strategy with their families. This needs to be done 5, 10, and 15 years away from the retirement of the owner so that everything is out in the open. The family needs to talk about their goals, not only for the business, but for themselves. Talk about what needs to happen to ensure that what is of critical importance to the family stays that way. How can you work as a team and build off of each other's strengths? How can you grow mutual respect amongst the siblings or family members, so that the business becomes a source of mutual delight? What boundaries need to be set? What works in your family and what doesn't?

B. **Bring In The Professionals:** This doesn't just mean lawyers and accountants (though these are important). Consider mediators, business coaches, and even family therapists to develop conflict resolution skills and mediation techniques so that your family is prepared for any difficulties that you will face.

C. **Consider Your Other Options:** Maybe, after discussion with your family or business professionals, or after reading these pages, you are having second thoughts. Consider other options for your business. Perhaps, instead of giving the business to family members you might elect to have a board of directors or a professional management team run the business and your family members act as shareholders. Don't just think about your business assets but your whole portfolio. Could you divide your possessions in such a way that you will be able to minimize the strife caused to your family? Can you get agreement now to prevent disagreements in the future?

If your family needs help in this area, a great resource in North America is the Galliard Family Business Advisors Institute, which can be found on the net at https://galliardinstitute.org/. This organization will put you in touch with experts who can help your family transition from one generation to the next. They have expertise in strategic and succession planning, family charters, operating agreements, advisory board development, and executive coaching.

Selling the Business

When I start working with business owners, they often want to know how much their business is worth. Many owners have dreams of retiring and selling their business for 1 million dollars or another price they think it is worth. Yet, in many cases, these same business owners have not taken the time to create value in their business so that it is saleable. After we talk about it for a few minutes, they understand that, in some cases, they are just selling a job or, worse yet, just the inventory. Who really wants to buy a business where everything is dependent on the current owner or a business that is barely paying the owner wages? These are exactly the same reasons the current owner is asking me what it is worth and thinking of getting out.

To create a business that has value, business owners need to think strategically. Whether you want to sell your business tomorrow or in 5 year's time, there are certain things that buyers are looking for. These include:

Profits and Cash Flow: Buyers need profits. If your business is only making marginal profits, you need to look at a variety of strategies that work to increase profitability. A business without profits has no or little value. If you are taking profit out of your business in ways other than cash, you need to ensure that everything is in the books if you want to maximize your business's selling price. Additionally, you need to think about how you are taking cash out of the company. A fair portion of the cash you are taking out of the business for your personal use needs to be put down as management costs if you are involved in the management of your business. This allows the buyers of the business to fairly assess where they can trim costs and generate profits.

Recurring Revenue: If you can prove to prospective business buyers that you have a model of free cash flow and/or recurring revenue, you have a winner. Buyers want to see that your customers are returning on a regular basis and that you have systematic ways of tracking their return. In other words, if you have a subscription-based model or clients that buy every quarter, month, week, or day, you will receive more money for your business than someone who is reliant on one-off sales.

Buyers are also looking for a business that they don't need to feed cash. In other words, by improving your cash flow, you can increase the value of your business. You can do this in a number of ways;

the easiest way is to reduce your inventory and ensure that your receivables are in a manageable state. The less your receivables are overdue, the more likely you are to sell at a higher price.

Growth Potential: People buy businesses because: 1) they believe that they can make more money by improving your systems or reducing your costs, and 2) they believe they can generate more growth. If you can prove that your business is replicable either in new geographic markets or to new niche markets, you have a winner. Start thinking outside the box as to how your business could be grown, even if you are not planning to grow it there. You need to remember that the buyer of your business is just starting out and needs to believe that they can explode out of the starting gate and get phenomenal returns on their investment.

A Focused Business: Keep your pedal to the metal. Sometimes, when business owners think of selling, they lose focus and start gearing down. This is a big mistake because buyers are looking for businesses that are growing. When a business starts to decline, it is difficult to turn the ship around. Keeping your business in tip-top shape, continuing to focus on marketing and differentiation, and creating value for the customer can make a huge difference to prospective buyers.

Systems: Many business owners are proud because they know everything that goes on in their business. They know the customers by name, they negotiate all the deals with the suppliers, and they hire and fire the staff. This is all wonderful if you are planning to run the business until the day you die, but if you want to sell the business, your value only increases when you can step back and start delegating all of these aspects of the business. A business that makes money and isn't reliant on the owner is more valuable than a business that has customers who have come to rely on talking about their problems with the business owner on a daily basis. A business that doesn't rely on the owner being there, but has a team that can run the company, gives the buyer two options:

1. They can run the company themselves and eliminate the manager in order to make more money.

2. They can run the company with the team and get a return on their investment for little or no work.

Increasing Your Potential for Sale of Your Business?

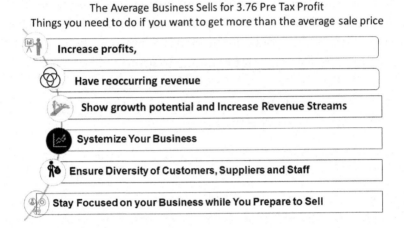

The Average Business Sells for 3.76 Pre Tax Profit
Things you need to do if you want to get more than the average sale price

Increase profits,

Have reoccurring revenue

Show growth potential and Increase Revenue Streams

Systemize Your Business

Ensure Diversity of Customers, Suppliers and Staff

Stay Focused on your Business while You Prepare to Sell

Build It To Sell it!

In his book, *Built to Sell*, John Warrillow says businesses that are more specialized and have a variety of customers, sell for a higher value than those that sell commodity products to a smaller amount of customers.

Even if we don't want to sell our business right now, as owners, we should be looking at reducing our workload so that our business doesn't get stuck in the daily grind. Buyers want businesses with systems. This allows the new owners to follow the operations procedures even when you are not there to train them. The simpler and clearer the systems, the higher value you have created. To generate more value in our business, we need systems that work so that our employees know exactly what to do and when to do it, each and every day of the year. Setting planning structures in place for marketing, sales, automation, and innovation ensures that the business will be vibrant and viable without our input as owners.

How Much is Your Business Worth?

This is the 'Million Dollar Question' that every business owner is thinking about at some point. Lets face it, as owners, we put our blood, sweat, and tears into our operations. We spend countless hours, energy, money, and ideas into building our 'empire.' We have even lost out on other opportunities because we have been focused on building the business. It must be worth something. You have probably heard of many different ways of valuing a business:

- Actual value (your assets minus your liabilities or anything you owe)

- Multiples of sales (take your sales figure and times it by the agreed upon rate)

- Discounted cash flow (potential cash flow discounted by the interest rate in today's dollars)

- Multiples of profit (profit of the business times an agreed upon multiplier)

- Percentage of annual sales (common in some industries)

Here are the hard facts. According to John Warrillow, most businesses sell for 3.76 times their pre-tax profit (EBITA for those of you with a financial brain). In other words, if your business is making $100,000 per year in pre-tax profit, it will probably sell for around $376,000 (Warrillow, 2016). This final sale price depends on the industry, economy, and a number of factors related to the business, as we stated before. However, the range for most small business sales is 2.76 to 6.27 times the pre-tax profit. Again, we see the need for your business to make a profit. This pre-tax profit is often taken as an average from the previous two or three yearly financial statements. If you have figured out ways of reducing your profit to reduce your taxes, you need to start ensuring that your financial statements correctly reflect how much profit that you are making.

Rule Of Thumb

Tom West is another leading expert when it comes to business valuation. His company, Business Brokerage Press, just completed its 26th year of publishing valuation books. As a business broker and author with over 30 years of experience, Tom has written a number of books on business valuation and has come up with the Rule of Thumb principal. **This Rule of Thumb is the down and dirty way of figuring out roughly how much your business is worth.** While there are a number of factors that influence the final selling price of any business, Tom West says that the Rule of Thumb is based on selling information from business brokers across North America. With this information, you can get a pretty good idea of how much a given business will sell for based on your location (West, 2016).

Here are some examples of how different types of business are valued:

Accounting Firms	100-125% of annual revenues
Auto Dealers (New Cars)	0-10% of annual sales + inventory
Bookstores	15% of annual sales + inventory
Coffee Shops (Gourmet)	40% of annual sales + inventory
Day Care Centres	40-50% of annual sales + inventory
Dental Practices	60-65% of annual revenues + inventory
Dry Cleaners	70-80% of annual sales + inventory
Engineering Services	40-45% of annual services

Flower Shops	30-35% of annual sales + inventory
Food Shops (Gourmet)	30% of annual sales + inventory
Gas Stations (without Convenience Store)	15-20% of annual sales + inventory
Gift/Card Shops	35% of annual sales + inventory
Grocery Stores	15% of annual sales + inventory
Hardware Stores	45% of annual sales + inventory
Insurance Agencies	125-150% of annual revenues
Landscape Businesses	45% of annual sales
Law Practices	90-100% of annual revenues
Liquor Stores	40-45% of annual sales + inventory
Restaurants (Full-serve)	30-35% of annual sales + inventory
Restaurants (Limited-serve	30-40% of annual sales + inventory
Sporting Good Stores	25% of annual sales + inventory
Taverns/Bars	40% of annual sales + inventory
Travel Agencies	35-40% of annual commissions
Veterinary Practices	70% of annual revenues + inventory
Source: Business Brokerage Press https://business-brokeragepress.com	

The sale of any business is determined by the willingness of what a buyer is prepared to pay based their valuation of that business and how much of a rush the business owner is in to sell the business. Making your business valuable to buyers takes time and preparation, but if you are willing to do it you can reap the rewards. The sooner you can plan for your exit and the sale of the business, the more likely you will have success when that time comes. Take some time right now and make a few notes for yourself.

When do you think you would like to exit your business?

What will be the factors that will influence that decision?

What is your plan for leaving the business? Will you shut it down, sell it, pass it on to family members, put a manager in and continue to run it, or something else? Write it down.

How much money do you need to get from your business to retire in the fashion that you would like?

What are the things that you need to do to ensure that you will get the money you need and deserve when you sell the business. List 5 things:

1.

2.

3.

4.

5.

Who are three people you need to talk to or hire to ensure that you get the maximum value for your business:

1.

2.

3.

What other information do you need?

Chapter References (BDC, 2016) (Warrilow, 2010)
http://www.bizstats.com./reports/sole-proprietor-labor-costs.php

Health Tip for Business Owners: Worried about Forgetting Things as You Age?

There is some research to show that doing puzzles or brain teasers on a regular basis can help your memory as you age. In addition, healthy fats like coconut oil and omega 3 oil from salmon and other fish can make a difference in brain function and memory! We all age and the stress of a business can speed up the aging process. Slow it down by doing challenging things that bring you joy!

Chapter 15: The Big Adventure

Live the dream and make the world a
better place with your profits.

The Big Adventure

I first met Henry when I was about 14 years old when my mom was buying a goat from him, but that is a story better told by her! Henry Gilbert is an inspiration and a character that you should meet if you ever get the chance. At 80 years of age and full of wisdom, Henry views life from a different lens than anybody else I know. As a young man, Henry had a life of adventure; an Englishman born in India, he had worked for Jaguar as a mechanic before he came to Canada, met the love of his life (Catherine) in Vancouver, and moved north for opportunity. One day, when he was working as a heavy-duty mechanic to support his large family, the boss came in and said someone was going to be laid off. Seeing another man who had a family who would be facing the unemployment line and desperation, Henry volunteered his job instead. To feed his own family,

Henry had a number of ventures and contracts, from logging, reforestation, and operating government campsites. Money never has held much allure for Henry. Henry had some good times but wasn't rich.

I dropped in to see Henry just the other day as I was on my way to a farm to purchase some cattle to sell as beef in our stores. We had a coffee and talked as we sat in the sunshine outside his log cabin. Henry laughed as he told me about a recent incident when he called the ambulance because he thought he was having a stroke when he woke up one morning.

"I realized just a couple miles down the road, Dave," he said, *"that I was just dizzy and didn't have a stroke, but how do you tell the ambulance driver to turn around and drop you back home? So, I played along. I got to the hospital and did all the tests. My wife said I had a brain tumour and my kids thought I was dying, but I knew I was fine. As I lay there on the bed, though, I started thinking about all the adventures I have had in life. It came to me then that the next chapter, what happens after we die, is really the big adventure! No one knows what is going to happen, and that is what makes it so exciting, and I guess scary for some people."*

Synopsis

Reading this book is a bit like life. You are at the end in a couple of pages and the next chapter is up to you. What happens next is totally going to be written by you and your decisions to move your business forward!

The Adventure of a Restaurant Owner

Pam's restaurant was a problem for her. At one time, she thought it was an adventure, but now she was working too much and not making enough money. Pam's problems were rooted in the fact that she was trying to be all things to all people. On a personal level, she was trying to be a mom, wife, friend, and parent support at her kid's school. On a business level, Pam was literally the chief cook and bottle washer; she had her fingers in everything from ordering to scheduling. Pam was run ragged! She had done a wonderful job in getting her business to a certain level of sales, but the success was killing her! What could she do to get rid of the stress outside of eliminating the business? Pam needed help.

Pam's first change was to make sure that she was paid fairly for what she did. Pam decided that she wanted to make five thousand dollars a month for her efforts (up two thousand from what she was taking home). Pam also decided that she needed to set personal and business goals for herself and wanted to be held accountable to them. Those goals included tripling the annual profit, putting systems in place so she didn't have to do as much work, and scheduling her time so that the restaurant wasn't a ball and chain. To move towards her goals, Pam did the following:

1. Made a list of those tasks that she didn't want to do anymore and started training and delegating those jobs.

2. Held required monthly staff meetings. She used these sessions for training (including sales training for her servers).

3. Implemented strategic planning afternoons once a quarter with her key staff to decide what needed to be fixed and how to do it.

4. Asked her bookkeeper for monthly financial statements. She started monitoring KPIs including food costs, gross margins, customer counts per hour, average sales, and other metrics.

5. Focused on her key niche markets and stopped some of her generic advertising. She added a couple theme nights per month and improved the atmosphere in her restaurant.

6. Introduced a smaller menu, focusing on higher-margin, higher-quality offerings.

The Results!

In fewer than 12 months, Pam's sales increased by more than 35%! Because she was focused on higher margins and better buying, her expenses dropped and her gross margin increased by 6%. After her sales seminar for her servers, Pam noticed that her average sale increased and her tip pool grew! This resulted in a lower staff turnover rate as they were making more money. Staff commented that it was now more 'fun' to work in the restaurant and that Pam seemed 'less intense.' Despite Pam taking home more money as a salary, her bottom line increased. In fact, Pam's profit more than tripled and, as a result, the value of her business increased by fourfold!

On a personal level, Pam has her life back; she doesn't work as much in the business but, when she does work, she focuses more on working 'on her business' and how to improve it. Pam now has a business that is valuable and that she can sell. She is having much more fun and joked that she is in no rush now to rid herself of the 'ball and chain' any time soon.

This is how a business should work! A business is meant to make you money and provide you with a lifestyle that you enjoy. By putting into practice some of the things that Pam has done with her business (just like those listed in this book), you can have a business that is profitable, valuable, and fun. The decision to improve your business is up to you. Many others have been exactly where your business is today and have made the decision to seek adventures and opportunities, to improve and become more profitable and more valuable. Are you going to stay where you are or are you going to be one of the 'successful' business owners who have a life outside their business?

What Are You Going To Do With All Those Profits, Better Health, And That Extra Time?

You are in business to make a profit and have a life. It is no use making a ton of money and working your days away tied as a slave to your business. Remember: your business should be a lifestyle, not a life sentence, so hopefully you can frame it that way. If you have gone through this book, you have discovered ways that you can improve the profitability of your business, reduce your stress, and have extra time for yourself. The big question is, what are you going to do with that time, money and energy? Of course this is up to you, but having a plan and using these resources wisely can make a huge difference in how you look, act and feel.

Do It Now!

Commit to Change: By working in a diligent manner on a regular basis and focusing on one area per month, you will be able to improve your profitability significantly over the period of one year. You may even be able to double or triple your profits as many of my clients have. The key is to know what you want and to determine how you are going to get there. **Are you going to make the commitment and stick with it?**

Set Aside Time

You should now also be aware that smart business owners have systems in place that allow them to work less and make more! This will reduce your stress and improve your health. Your road to success will be littered with mistakes, but learning from those mistakes and putting systems in place so that your staff can avoid those pitfalls will allow you to run your business from a distance with little time and energy involved. To do this, you must have a plan developed for where you want your business to be in the future. Have a plan for growth. It is essential that you have personal goals and dreams that you have written down shared with other people! You need to develop operations manuals and roles and responsibilities for your employees with accountability checks. Putting time in early to work on your business will ensure that you are not chained to the business in time. **Make time each week to work on your business. When will that be?**

Investing your Profits for a Better Future.

What to do with the profits you make is totally up to you but, as we talked about earlier, as a business owner, you don't have the retirement funds that you would have if you worked for government or a big corporation. It is up to you to provide for your retirement. Many business owners think that they are going to sell their business and retire in fashion. The truth, is this rarely happens as imagined. **By making profits on a monthly and yearly basis and reinvesting those profits in your business, you will be taken care of through residual income. You will have nest eggs that will provide you with the money you need to take care of yourself and your family as you age.** You will also have money to share with those around you that need that money to help make the world a better place. **It is a proven fact that those people that give generously of their time and money rarely are in need.** Try being more generous with your money and reap the rewards. You will feel better about yourself, and you will be making a difference in the lives of others.

Check out the documentary, *I Am*. It's the story of the famous movie producer Tom Shadyac who came to the realization after a near death experience that more money doesn't make people happier. He realized he was no happier (and perhaps less happier) in his 7000 square-foot mansion than he was when he had nothing. His argument is that the further we are from a community of others, the higher our degree of loneliness is. The big houses we live in, the riches that separate us from those who have nothing, and the isolation we create by focusing on ourselves, inhibit our happiness. I don't want to tell you the whole story, but one of the key take-aways for me was that **we are hardwired for a compassionate response to the distress of others and, by sharing our gifts, our talents, our money, and our experiences with others, our lives become more joy-filled, more fun, and more meaningful.** Who would like more joy, more fun, and more meaning in business? I know lots of business owners who would love more of those things.

As small business owners, we are ingrained in the community around us, with our customers, our families, and our passions. We see the needs and desires of other people in the community around us. As we become more profitable, more successful, and wealthier, we must not forget where we came from and where we are going. In his book, *Get Your Business to Work – 7 steps to earning more, working less and living the life you want*, George Hedley says it well... we must not postpone our lives and our families for business. He says that the most successful people are the most generous people: generous with time, money, and service. In other words, "give to the world the best you have and the best will come back to you."

So that brings us to the end of this book and the start of your adventure in tuning up your business. I sincerely hope that this book will help you make healthy profits and that you earn more and worry less. I would love to hear your stories!

Health Tip for Business Owners: Reduce Your Stress By Living In The Moment!

By focusing on 1 thing at a time, you are more likely to reduce your stress and get more done.

Research shows that being present to what you are doing helps you relax and avoid being overwhelmed!

About the Author

Dave Fuller has an entrepreneurial drive that has helped him start and run successful small businesses for over three decades. When he is not working on his businesses that employ over 30 people and achieved sales in the millions of dollars, Dave engages with other small business owners as a business coach to help them achieve profitability, success, and balance in their lives.

Dave's expertise is backed by his MBA, but is based on his real world experiences of growing and running his small businesses from the ground up. He has co-founded grassroots organizations and run successful environmental campaigns for better quality air and water. Dave has a proven ability to develop strategies that work for businesses and a track record of success with his clients.

Despite having a variety of business interests, Dave maintains balance in his life and loves to spend time with his beautiful wife, Margaret, and their four children. He believes in supporting people and organizations that are trying to make a difference in the world and in the past had a wide variety of board experience. He plays guitar in his church choir and his personal time is spent cycling, skiing, and socializing with his community of friends.

Besides managing his businesses, Dave owns Fuller Business Development and is a popular speaker for companies, associations, and trade groups who are trying to raise the business acumen of their members.

To contact Dave about speaking at your event, for help with your business, or just to comment on his book, email dave@profityourselfhealthy.com

To sign up for Dave's free monthly newsletter with tips on how to continuously improve your business, visit www.profityourselfhealthy.com

To download your Profit Yourself Healthy worksheets, go to www.profityourselfhealthy.com/bookdownloads/

Grateful Acknowledgements

This book would never have been written without the encouragement and support of so many people, and I would like to express my heartfelt thanks to them. I wish to start by thanking my wife Margaret who has been the joy of my life from the time I met her, and who has believed in me and my many projects when I often doubted myself. I couldn't have written this without her. I am also thankful for my parents, Roy and Diane, who brought me up to be curious, compassionate, and caring by their example, and showed me how working hard and thinking differently can make a difference. I am grateful for my siblings, staff, friends, and in-laws who all think I am crazy at times, but don't verbalize it very often. They have allowed me to use them to test ideas and points of view and have patiently supported projects as they came to fruition over time. I spent many hours writing this book that took away from time with my children whom I love dearly, Emily, Isabel, Sophia and Caleb. I appreciate the patience they had during this time and the belief that their dad could write a book.

Books need ideas, and this one is about business ideas. Without the support over the years from my partners, Louis and Rolande Matte, who took the chance on me in 1988 and invited me to join them in a start-up retail adventure, I might have had many less business experiences. I also need to thank the investors and partners in my various entrepreneurial activities who trusted me with their money and enabled me to try my wings in different businesses. Thank you to my instructors in college and university who challenged me to think outside of the box. Thank you to my coaching clients who shared with me their stories and allowed me to journey with them in their organizations for periods of time and from whom many of the stories in this book came from.

Jon Denny of the Professional Business Coaches Alliance PBCA invited me to join his organization, and that has changed my direction in life. The coaches that I have met through the PBCA included some authors who have been generous in sharing their knowledge about producing a book: Robert Sher, author of *Mighty Midsized Companies*, George Hedley who wrote *Get Your Business to Work* Jim Horan of the *One Page Plan*. Jim gave me "permission' to be irreverent in my writing and took time to listen. I appreciate the time that Roland Gahler, Lisë Stewart, Tom West, Dave Lee, and others I interviewed for this book have given me. Finally I have my own business coach Dennis Bonagara who has been a great mentor, coach and friend. I look forward to our weekly conversations where he challenges me and shares his great wisdom. He has helped moved this project forward through his regular contributions and ability to keep me accountable.

There are many book details that I didn't know about, and I appreciate the contributions made by my editors Geoffrey Boyd, Jodi Robertson, and also by Donncha O'Callaghan, who spent many hours cleaning up my writing. Tim, Jordan, and Raeanne at Tellwell for all their help and guidance.

Finally, I am thankful for my life and the Creator that gave that life to me. I have been blessed and surrounded with wonderful opportunities, incredible beauty, and unbelievably good people whom I have been fortunate to share this journey of life with. For all of this, I am truly grateful.

Reference List

American Psychological Association. (2015). Stress in America. *Washington DC: APA.*

Anderson, S. (2003). Effects of $9 price endings on Retail Sales. Quantitative Marketing and Economics Journal, *93-110.*

Ariely, D. (2008). Predictably Irrational. *Harpercollins.*

BDC. (2016). Selling Your Business - Seven steps to increase value. Business Development Corp.

Canada, G. o. (2013, August). Key Small Business Statistics. *Retrieved from Industry Canada: https://www.ic.gc.ca/eic/site/061.nsf/vwapj/ KSBS-PSRPE_August-Aout2013_eng.pdf/$FILE/KSBS-PSRPE_ August-Aout2013_eng.pdf*

Carnegie, D. (1936). How to Win Friends and Influence People. *New York: Pocket Books.*

Chevalier, M. (2012). Luxury Brand Management. *Wiley.*

Dickenson, S. (1990). The Price Knowledge and Search of Supermarket Shoppers. Journal of Marketing, *42-53.*

Farris, P. (2010). Marketing Metrics. *Upper Saddle River, NJ: Pearson Education.*

Financial-Projections.com. (2016). Butler Consultants Free Industry Statistics. *http://research.financial-projections.com/IndustryStats-Name.shtml.*

Flynn, A. (2012). Custom Nation. *BENBELLA Books.*

Gahler, R. (2016, February 26th). *Phone call interview. (D. Fuller, Interviewer)*

Hall, D. (2001). Jump Start Your Business Brain. *Eureka Institute.*

Hedley, G. (2009). Get Your Business to Work. *Ben Bella Books.*

Holtz, H. (1996). *Priced to Sell; A complete Guide to More Profitable Pricing. Upstart Publishing.*

Kanter, R. M. (2011 November). *How Great Companies Think Differently.* Harvard Review.

Kolter, K. C. (2007). A Framework for Marketing Management. *Toronto: Pearson.*

Mate, D. G. (2004). When Your Body Says No. *Vintage Canada.*

Matthews, D. G. (2007). *The impact of commitment, accountablity and written goals on achievements.* 87th Convention of the Western Psychological Association. *Vancouver, B.C.*

NFIB/Wells Fargo "Business Stop and Starts Series" 1999

Oxfam. (2015, January 29th). Wealth Having it all and Wanting More. *Retrieved from Oxfam International: http://policy-practice.oxfam.org. uk/publications/wealth-having-it-all-and-wanting-more-338125*

Parkes, D. (2016, September). *No Margin No Mission.* Canadian National Health Retailer.